PRAISE FOR
EMPOWERED TO LEAD

Dr. Wilson has given the global church a profound gift in *Empowered to Lead*. With clarity, conviction, and a lifetime of Spirit-filled experience, he speaks into the leadership vacuum of our generation and offers a Christ-centered, Spirit-empowered way forward. This is not simply another book on leadership; it is a call to integrity, servanthood, and bold vision that resonates deeply with the heart of God for His people today. Every pastor, leader, and believer aspiring to influence their world for Christ will find in these pages wisdom that is both timeless and urgently relevant. I wholeheartedly commend this book to you.

—Glyn Barrett
Senior Pastor, !Audacious Church; National Director, Assemblies of God Great Britain

Dr. Wilson is one of the greatest leaders I know. *Empowered to Lead* should be required reading for every leader and anyone aspiring to lead in any sphere of life. This book is full of invaluable leadership wisdom and practical application.

—Christine Caine
Founder, A21 and Propel Women

Understanding that effective leadership in the twenty-first century is critical, Dr. Wilson has given us *Empowered to Lead*. The ability to adapt to societal challenges is a constant learning experience. Dr. Wilson combines his life experiences and knowledge of the Spirit's work in the life of a leader to give us a resource that will help leaders turn their vision into reality.

—Doug Clay
General Superintendent, Assemblies of God USA

I have known Dr. Billy Wilson for a number of years now and had the privilege of seeing the impact he's had on countless thousands of lives around the globe, mine included. *Empowered to Lead* is essential for every believer who desires to make a lasting impact on the world. It serves as a road map for leaders across every sphere of influence. With clarity and conviction, Dr. Billy Wilson equips believers to lead with boldness, integrity, and Spirit-empowered vision. Read it, live it, and watch as God raises up leaders who will bring godly transformation to our world.

—Russell Evans
Senior Pastor, Planetshakers

In his new book, Dr. Billy Wilson captures something vital—we're not facing a leadership crisis but an incredible leadership opportunity. *Empowered to Lead* provides a practical road map for developing the five essential qualities every Spirit-empowered leader needs. Having witnessed these principles transform thousands of students in his role as president of ORU, Billy knows how ordinary people become extraordinary leaders. For anyone ready to grow their leadership capacity, this book delivers.

—Bobby Gruenewald
Founder and CEO, YouVersion

Empowered to Lead provides a robust framework for Spirit-empowered leadership, combining theological depth with practical wisdom. Dr. Billy Wilson demonstrates that true leadership is transformational, grounded in character, and sustained by Holy Spirit dependence. His insights on resilience—learning to lead even when "injured"—are indispensable for today's leaders. This book is a valuable guide for educators, executives, and ministry leaders seeking to cultivate integrity, perseverance, and Spirit-led impact in their spheres of influence.

—Dr. Wayne Hilsden
President, King of Kings Ministries and
Fellowship of Israel Related Ministries (FIRM)

Empowered to Lead reignites your passion for living out your purpose by refueling your faith. With the seasoned wisdom of a lifelong leader and Christ follower, Dr. Billy Wilson inspires leaders at every level with insight curated by experience. He reveals how our relationship with the Holy Spirit uniquely equips us to lead beyond our own abilities. If leadership seems more like a burden than a blessing, let *Empowered to Lead* recharge your attitude toward faith as well as followers.

—Chris Hodges
Chancellor, Highlands College; Founding Pastor, Church of the Highlands; Author, *Pray First* and *Breathe Again*

Empowered to Lead is a timely and Spirit-filled road map for today's leadership moment. Dr. Billy Wilson reminds us that authentic leadership isn't about titles or influence but about being empowered by the Holy Spirit to serve with integrity, courage, and vision. In a world desperate for godly leaders, this book issues a clear call: The opportunity is before us, and we must answer it.

—Rob Hoskins
Cofounder and President, OneHope

Empowered to Lead is a road map for a new generation. Dr. Wilson exemplifies the truths of servant leadership he writes about in this extraordinary book. In the coming great revivals, every believer needs to try to reach their full potential for lasting transformation. This book will get you to that mark.

—Dr. Cindy Jacobs
Generals International

Empowered to Lead is a wonderful book! Like its author, it is profound yet practical, providing a toolbox while offering a most vulnerable glimpse into the journey of a leader. One of the great insights is that true influence is found not in perfection but in faithfulness. This encouraging book will undoubtedly serve as an invaluable resource for anyone who desires to be a leader not just of people but of transformation—all through the empowering presence of the Holy Spirit.

—Bill Johnson
Senior Leader, Bethel Church, Redding, California;
Author, *Removing the Sting of Death* and *God Is Good*

When I think of Spirit-led leaders in modern evangelical circles, one that rises to the top is Dr. Billy Wilson. As he has demonstrated throughout his ministry, Dr. Wilson epitomizes what it means to be a servant leader while communicating the message of leadership in whatever project, ministry, event, or initiative he leads. *Empowered to Lead* promises to be a guide that rising Spirit-filled leaders will find a must-read.

—Gary J. Lewis
General Overseer, Church of God

Few voices carry the authority and authenticity of Dr. Billy Wilson when it comes to Spirit-empowered leadership. In *Empowered to Lead*, Dr. Wilson not only addresses today's leadership crisis but also presents a clear path forward from the heart of a father to this generation. His vision of leadership is grounded in character and ignited by the Spirit. This is more than a theory; it is practical, biblical, and urgently needed. Every pastor, evangelist, and emerging leader should take these lessons to heart and apply them for the sake of the gospel.

—Nathan Morris
Founder and President, Shake the Nations Ministries;
Cochairman, Global Evangelist Alliance

This insightful book offers a comprehensive, in-depth, clear, and practical guide to leadership. Dr. Wilson covers essential aspects of leadership with engaging and powerful examples and testimonies from Scripture, global influencers, and personal reflections. It's ideal for first-time leaders seeking purpose and understanding, while also sharpening the vision of seasoned leaders. For those discouraged and failed leaders, it brings renewed passion and direction. At its heart, this book reveals Dr. Wilson's deep desire to raise a new generation of Spirit-empowered leaders—leaders equipped to make a lasting, Christ-centered impact on the world.

—Dr. Niko Njotorahardjo
Senior Pastor, GBI Jl. Jend. Gatot Subroto, Jakarta

As board chair of ORU, I saw these principles lived out from the front row. *Empowered to Lead* is not theory; it's a behind-the-scenes look at spiritual leadership in action. This book is timely and practical, and will inspire a new generation to lead with boldness and faith.

—Dr. Mike Rakes
Fifth president, Evangel University; Author,
The Black Start Leader: Reigniting Power and Purpose When Everything Goes Dark

The world is crying out for authenticity and a deep, abiding sense of purpose. As Christians we are called not just to participate in this pursuit but to lead it. *Empowered to Lead* by Dr. Wilson equips people of faith to do just that, providing a guide to understanding and undertaking the journey of Spirit-filled leadership. This book was developed through decades of leadership experience, and everyone, regardless of their role or responsibilities, will benefit from Dr. Wilson's wisdom and perspective.

—Pastor Samuel Rodriguez
Lead Pastor, New Season

What an edifying, powerful book. Every Spirit-filled leader should read it.

—Larry Stockstill, DD
Founder and Director, Pastors University

Multigenerational leaders with kingdom qualities of leadership are developed by the multiple experiences and influences that shape them. In *Empowered to Lead,* Dr. Billy Wilson vividly portrays the experiences, convictions, and influences that have shaped him to be the multigenerational kingdom leader he is today. As fellow leaders, we do well to read and apply.

—Rev. David Wells, MA, DD
Vice-Chairman, Pentecostal World Fellowship; General Superintendent, The Pentecostal Assemblies of Canada; President, Pentecostal Charismatic Churches of North America

EMPOWERED TO LEAD

OTHER TITLES BY DR. BILLY WILSON

*As the Waters Cover the Sea: The Story of
Empowered21 and the Movement It Serves
(coauthored with the late Vinson Synan)*

Generation Z: Born for the Storm

The Power of One: Reaching Every Person on Earth

*Fasting Forward: Advancing Your
Spiritual Life Through Fasting*

*Father Cry: Healing Your Heart and
the Hearts of Those You Love*

FOREWORD BY DAVID GREEN OF HOBBY LOBBY

DR. BILLY WILSON

PRESIDENT OF ORAL ROBERTS UNIVERSITY

EMPOWERED TO LEAD

BECOMING A LEADER WHO IMPACTS THE WORLD

Empowered Books
An imprint of ORU Press

Empowered to Lead: Becoming a Leader Who Impacts the World by Dr. Billy Wilson
Copyright © 2026 Oral Roberts University
orupress.org

All rights reserved. No part of this book may be used or reproduced in any way whatsoever without written permission, except in the case of brief quotations in critical articles and reviews. For more information, contact ORU Press, 7777 S. Lewis Ave., Tulsa, OK 74171 USA.

Empowered Books, an imprint of ORU Press, is a registered trademark of Oral Roberts University Press.

Published by Harp & Sword Media LLC
Cover design by Oral Roberts University

Unless otherwise noted, all Scripture quotations are taken from the Holy Bible, New International Version®, NIV®. Copyright © 1973, 1978, 1984, 2011 by Biblica, Inc.® Used by permission of Zondervan. All rights reserved worldwide. www.zondervan.com. The "NIV" and "New International Version" are trademarks registered in the United States Patent and Trademark Office by Biblica, Inc.®

Scripture quotations marked AMP are from the Amplified® Bible (AMP), Copyright © 2015 by The Lockman Foundation. Used by permission. www.Lockman.org.

Scripture quotations marked KJV are from the King James Version of the Bible.

Scripture quotations marked NLT are taken from the *Holy Bible*, New Living Translation, copyright ©1996, 2004, 2015 by Tyndale House Foundation. Used by permission of Tyndale House Publishers, Carol Stream, Illinois 60188. All rights reserved.

While the publisher has made every effort to provide accurate internet addresses at the time of publication, neither the publisher nor the author assumes any responsibility for errors or for changes that occur after publication. Further, the publisher does not have any control over and does not assume any responsibility for author or third-party websites or their content.

ISBN (jacketed hardcover): 979-8-9997394-0-7
ISBN (ebook): 979-8-9997394-1-4

10 9 8 7 6 5 4 3 2 1

Printed in the United States of America

Dedication

This volume is dedicated to the next generation of Spirit-empowered leaders. Never in world history have leaders who are filled with the Holy Spirit and grounded in spiritual integrity been needed more. I desire that the students of Oral Roberts University will be these kinds of leaders and will impact every sphere of society for Jesus Christ. I pray that the words of this book will inspire them, along with thousands of other leaders around the world, to posture their hearts as servants and receive God's Spirit so they can be empowered to lead.

CONTENTS

Foreword by David Green xv

Acknowledgments xix

Introduction xxiii

CHAPTER 1	**FOUNDATIONS FOR LEADERSHIP** 1
CHAPTER 2	**THE LEADERSHIP STYLES OF JESUS** 9
CHAPTER 3	**LEADING BY THE SPIRIT** 23
CHAPTER 4	**LEADERSHIP AND THE GIFTS OF THE SPIRIT** 37
CHAPTER 5	**EMPOWERED BY SUPERNATURAL GIFTS** 61
CHAPTER 6	**THE HEART OF A LEADER** 77
CHAPTER 7	**LESSONS FROM A YOUNG LEADER** 87
CHAPTER 8	**CRITICAL ASSETS EVERY LEADER NEEDS** 101
CHAPTER 9	**HIDDEN GEMS FOR LEADERS** 115
CHAPTER 10	**PRINCIPLES OF LEADERSHIP**................. 123
CHAPTER 11	**SPIRIT-EMPOWERED LEADERS AND THEIR MOVEMENT** 137
CHAPTER 12	**HEALING IN LEADERSHIP**.................... 157
CHAPTER 13	**HANDLING FAILURE IN LEADERSHIP**........ 173
CHAPTER 14	**BECOMING A WHOLE LEADER** 187
CONCLUSION	**A SPIRIT-EMPOWERED LEADER: THE FULL PICTURE** 195

Notes... 199

FOREWORD

Leadership has always been one of the defining needs of every generation. In times of flourishing, strong and wise leaders are needed to steward momentum. In times of crisis, steady, Spirit-guided leaders bring clarity and hope. Today we live in a world that hungers for leadership marked not merely by talent or charisma but by integrity, resilience, and a deep dependence on God's Spirit. *Empowered to Lead* speaks directly into that longing.

Dr. Billy Wilson writes not as a distant theorist but as a leader who has walked the journey for decades—learning, serving, and mentoring others in nearly every sphere of society. These pages are not abstract principles pulled from leadership textbooks; they are lessons shaped by real people, real challenges, and real faith. That makes this book both timeless and timely—timeless because the foundations of leadership do not shift with trends, timely because the world is asking, sometimes desperately, for leaders who are different, leaders who embody character and conviction.

What struck me in reading this work is how thoroughly Dr. Wilson integrates the spiritual with the practical. Too often books on leadership focus only on strategies, management skills, or influence techniques. Those things have value, but they are not enough. At the same time, purely devotional reflections, while inspiring, can feel disconnected from the realities of leading people and organizations in today's complex world. This book refuses that false choice. Within these pages spiritual empowerment and practical wisdom are woven together so that the reader is equipped both to follow Christ closely and to lead others effectively.

The chapters take us from the foundations of leadership to the example of Jesus Himself, and then into the empowering work of the Holy Spirit. Readers will find careful exploration of leadership theories and models but always anchored in the conviction that leadership without the Spirit ultimately falls short. What makes this volume unique is its insistence that Spirit-filled leadership is not an optional dimension—it is essential if we want leadership that transforms rather than simply manages.

I was especially encouraged by the way Dr. Wilson lifts the next generation. At a time when cynicism about youth is common, this book sees in them extraordinary potential. It refuses to accept the narrative of decline and instead points to hope: young women and men rising with bold vision, grounded in integrity, and empowered by the Spirit of God to impact every sphere of society. For students, young professionals, or anyone wondering whether their life can truly make a difference, this resource will be an encouragement.

Yet the book is not only for emerging leaders. Seasoned leaders too will recognize themselves in its pages. Some sections will affirm what you have already learned in your own journey; others will gently confront and call you higher. In every chapter you will sense that God is not finished shaping us as leaders, no matter how long we've been serving. That humility—born from a lifetime of leadership, travel, and ministry—comes through in Billy's voice.

Reading *Empowered to Lead* left me with both conviction and hope—conviction because it is impossible to ignore the ways our world has settled for shallow or self-serving leadership, sometimes even within the church, and hope because the Spirit of God is still raising leaders who live differently, leaders who are marked by love, courage, resilience, and faith. This book is a resource, yes, but more than that it is a call.

My prayer for every reader is that you will not simply consume these words as information but receive them as an invitation. Let them stir you to deeper dependence on the Spirit. Let them remind you that your influence, whether great or small in the eyes of the world, matters profoundly in God's purposes. And let them encourage you to step boldly into the arena of leadership—not for your own glory but for the glory of the One who called you, equipped you, and empowers you still.

If you are ready to lead with integrity, courage, and the Spirit's power, then you hold in your hands more than a book. You hold a guide for the adventure ahead.

—David Green
CEO and Founder, Hobby Lobby

ACKNOWLEDGMENTS

I recently celebrated fifty years of being a Spirit-filled and empowered Christian. I have difficulty believing that fifty years have passed! During those years, I have traveled around the world, visiting more than one hundred nations and speaking in most of them. I have met leaders in a multitude of settings, from church, business, education, entertainment, and more. I have learned from all these leaders. Sometimes I have learned things that I absolutely wanted to emulate in my leadership, and at other times, things that I certainly did not want to emulate. Throughout all these encounters my leadership journey has been sharpened and affected by a multitude. I realized early on that leadership would be key in our generation, so I have tried throughout the years to read numerous books, articles, and more about leadership. I am certain that I internalized many things I read, and this will be evident in the writing of this book. To all those leaders and writers who will not be credited in this book, thank you for inspiring me, encouraging me, and at times even correcting me.

A variety of life circumstances and educational opportunities form leaders. We are always learning and adapting to be successful in leadership. Due to unique responsibilities, I have been extremely honored to meet some of God's exemplary, Spirit-empowered leaders of our generation—men and women far more advanced and gifted than me. Some of them were well-known, and others less known; nonetheless, they were mighty in God. I am incredibly grateful for all these opportunities to connect and fellowship with God's best.

Many people contribute to the process of writing books. First, I appreciate the Oral Roberts University Board of Trustees for allowing me time each summer to focus on study, research, and writing. Without this dedicated space each year, this volume would not have been possible. I also want to thank my immediate office staff. My executive assistant, Lisa Bowman, keeps my life schedule sane and intercedes for our work every single day. My executive administrator and personal assistant, Eric Peterson, serves me in amazing ways. He is a servant leader extraordinaire and has heard the lessons contained in this book more than any other person on earth. Ana Petrak serves our department with a sweet spirit and great efficiency. Most importantly for this project, I thank Alyssa Sanders, who coordinates all my writing projects, and who in this case did an amazing job of collecting my lectures from my Spirit-Empowered Leadership class and providing the basic structure for this book. Alyssa's contribution to this project cannot be overstated, as she has overseen editing, cover design, final copy, and distribution. Thank you, Alyssa. We are so proud of you!

The entire President's Cabinet at ORU served as cheerleaders for this project, encouraging me to complete it so that leaders around the world could benefit from the lessons I have learned. My Cabinet forms an amazing team that has successfully led various areas of our university with excellence. One of the great leadership lessons is that teamwork makes the dream work, and this could never be truer than with the present ORU Cabinet. Thank you to Dr. Kathaleen Reid-Martinez, provost; Neal Stenzel, CFO; Tim Philley, COO; Terry Kollmorgen, general counsel and executive adviser to the president; Dr. Charles Scott, VP of External Affairs; Mike Mathews, VP of Global Learning and Innovation; Mike Carter, VP of Development and Alumni Relations; Lori Cook, VP of Student Life; Alison Vujnovic, VP of Enrollment Management, and Tim Johnson, athletic director. All of you are amazing leaders, and I am honored to serve with you.

I am grateful to Kay Horner for editing this book, as she has edited nearly every book I have written! Her sound spiritual insight and keen editorial eye helped to smooth this manuscript and prepare it for the world. I also appreciate Harp & Sword Media, my partners in this journey, tasked with getting this book ready for market. Their encouragement and excellent work have been a great blessing.

My family has always been key to my leadership. My amazing wife, Lisa, has joined me in traveling around the world and served with me through these years of leadership. She has contributed far more than 50 percent to our success, and I am eternally grateful that she accepted my invitation to this life adventure. My two children, Ashley and Sara, are both great leaders in their areas of service. Ashley serves as the Empowered21 executive director, and Sara, along with her husband, Shaun, serve as missionaries and lead a ministry called Serving Paraguay. I am proud of the leaders they have become. Ashley has three children, all of whom are now attending ORU, and Sara has four. Her oldest is currently attending our university. Seven grandchildren are a huge blessing to Lisa and me. I see in each of them, Anna, Aaron, Amelia, Abi, Sammy, James, and Benjamin, future Spirit-empowered leaders. Their impact for Christ will far exceed mine, and my heart is pleased by this in every way.

Finally, I want to acknowledge Jesus Christ, the greatest leader I have ever known, studied, or been nurtured by. Jesus' example and His presence with me through the Holy Spirit have guided my leadership throughout my adult life. I could not, nor would I ever desire to, attempt this journey without Him or His Spirit. He is the ultimate Spirit-empowered leader, and only through Jesus Christ is this book possible.

—Dr. Billy Wilson

INTRODUCTION

We *are in a leadership crisis!* I have heard this despairing cry consistently for the past three decades. Whether in politics, business, education, or the religious world, the same mantra has been expressed repeatedly. "We need leaders, and we can't find enough of them. We have a crisis." I believe that what we have in the twenty-first century is a leadership opportunity more than a leadership crisis. The exciting news is that a new generation is now emerging that has the potential to answer this leadership need in every sphere of society. As the fourth president of Oral Roberts University (ORU), I walk among these developing leaders on our campus every day. This new, emerging generation is amazing! The lessons in this book are designed to equip them and any other age group (you are included) being called to step forward and fill the leadership vacuum of this day.

Successful leadership in the twenty-first century is more crucial than ever. As we navigate rapid technological advancements, global interconnectedness, and complex societal challenges, effective leadership must guide us through these transformative times. Leaders today must be adaptable, visionary, and equipped to handle the unprecedented challenges and opportunities before us.

> *Leaders today must be adaptable, visionary, and equipped to handle the unprecedented challenges and opportunities before us.*

Any observer easily recognizes that many organizations and communities struggle with a lack of direction, integrity, and inspiration from their leaders. This has created a pervasive sense of leadership crisis globally. Organizations and nations are crying out for leaders who will lead. They are desperate for leaders who rise above mediocrity to lead with servanthood, wisdom, integrity, courage, and compassion.

In response to the leadership crisis of the twenty-first century, an unprecedented opportunity has emerged for spiritually empowered leaders. These Spirit-empowered leaders will not only be skilled and knowledgeable in their field, but will also be guided by the tangible and intangible—the invisible yet empowering presence of the Holy Spirit. Spirit-empowered leaders are being equipped to transcend personal ambition and make a positive impact on the world, bringing hope, healing, and transformation.

At ORU we are committed to developing such leaders. I am honored to teach a class each semester that focuses on our mission "to develop Holy Spirit–empowered leaders through whole person education to impact the world." During the fall semester the class is called Spirit-Empowered Living and is principally populated by our incoming class of freshmen and transfer students. More than one thousand eager and enthusiastic students typically fill the class, which is designed to help us build a shared vocabulary around the Spirit-empowered life and to challenge students personally in their walk with Christ.

Building on this foundational Spirit-Empowered Living class, I teach a spring semester course called Spirit-Empowered Leadership. My spring course focuses on what it means to be a leader empowered by the Holy Spirit in the twenty-first century. I believe that every student attending ORU is a potential leader and that the Holy Spirit is essential to helping each one become all God has called them to be.

A few years ago our board of trustees, administration, faculty, and student focus groups asked the question "What qualities should a twenty-first-century Spirit-empowered leader possess?" Following months of synthesis and lots of prayer, we developed a new set of student outcomes for the university to embody these critical leadership attributes. Our students wanted these simplified into easy-to-remember statements of two words each. Therefore, ORU's present student outcomes are: *Spiritual Integrity, Personal Resilience, Intellectual Pursuit, Global Engagement,* and *Bold Vision.* In every area of the university, from the classroom to student life, we seek to develop these qualities in our students. I have been amazed by how wonderfully this leadership formation develops in the lives of our students since we have chosen to focus our energies on these outcomes. The growth I witness from their first days in the Spirit-Empowered Living and Leadership classes until I shake their hand on the commencement stage is incredible. They become whole leaders ready to change the world.

Our world desperately needs leaders who demonstrate godly qualities and are empowered by God's Spirit. If we are willing to focus our efforts and energies on developing those leaders in our generation, then world change is ahead. My prayer is that God will use this volume to help forge in you the characteristics needed to be a leader who will impact the world for the glory of God.

CHAPTER 1

FOUNDATIONS FOR LEADERSHIP

In the mid-1800s a lecture hall in London was filled with eager students. At the podium stood Thomas Carlyle, the fiery Scottish historian whose words carried the weight of authority. With dramatic conviction he declared, "The history of the world is but the biography of great men."[1]

Heads nodded and pens scratched against paper. For Carlyle and many of his contemporaries, leadership was destiny. History, he argued, was carried forward by towering leaders, the few remarkable individuals who shaped the world by their greatness, leaders such as Julius Caesar, Alexander the Great, Napoleon Bonaparte, William Shakespeare, and Martin Luther. Leadership was said to be reserved for the few—those born with innate genius and extraordinary qualities.

This "Great Man" theory dominated Western thought about leadership well into the early twentieth century. Universities taught it. Students believed it. Leaders justified their authority by it. The underlying assumption was that leaders are more born than made.

As the decades unfolded, cracks in this "Great Man" theory were revealed. Wars, revolutions, and social movements brought forward leaders who did not fit the mold. Research in psychology and sociology began questioning whether leadership was truly the exclusive domain of the innately gifted. Studies pointed to environment, opportunity, and development as key factors.[2] Leaders, it seemed, could also be developed. Now, generations later, the question remains: Are leaders born or made?

This question has been studied by scholars and researchers for decades, perhaps centuries, as leadership studies aim to determine whether leadership qualities and abilities are innate or shaped by various factors in a person's environment.

Research indicates that while some individuals may possess natural leadership traits, effective leadership can also be cultivated through experience, education, and personal development.[3]

In my opinion, some truth exists in both ideas. God has instilled gifting and potential inside each person. However, these gifts must be developed and refined through a variety of learning experiences. The work of the Holy Spirit is also vital in the developing and maturing process for a Spirit-empowered leader, who can make an effective, lasting impact in their sphere of influence.

> *The work of the Holy Spirit is vital in the developing and maturing process for a Spirit-empowered leader.*

DEFINITIONS OF LEADERSHIP

Defining *leadership* can be complex. It is a multifaceted concept with various definitions and perspectives. Some notable definitions include:

- **Peter Drucker:** "The only definition of a leader is someone who has followers."[4]
- **Kevin Kruse:** "Leadership is a process of social influence which maximizes the effort of others toward the achievement of a goal."[5]
- **Warren Bennis:** "Leadership is the capacity to translate vision into reality."[6]
- **John Maxwell:** "Leadership is influence; nothing more, nothing less."[7]
- **Murray Johannsen:** "Managers have subordinates. Leaders have followers."[8]
- **The US Air Force:** "Leadership is the art and science of influencing and directing people to accomplish the assigned mission."[9]
- **Martin Luther King Jr.:** "A genuine leader is not a searcher for consensus but a molder of consensus."[10]

- **Dwight D. Eisenhower:** "The essence of leadership is to get others to do something because they think you want it done and because they know it is worthwhile doing."[11]

At its core, leadership involves impact and not merely position. True leaders inspire, empower, shoulder responsibility, and press forward through adversity. Leaders are change agents; however, people dislike change, so leaders are often criticized. This is a part of leadership. President Teddy Roosevelt famously said:

> It is not the critic who counts; not the man who points out how the strong man stumbled, or where the doer of deeds could have done better. The credit belongs to the man who is actually in the arena, whose face is marred by dust and sweat and blood; who strives valiantly, who errs and comes short again and again, who knows the great enthusiasm, the great devotions, who spends himself in a worthy cause, who at best knows in the end the triumph of high achievement, and who, at the worst if he fails, at least fails while daring greatly, so that his place shall never be with those timid souls who know neither victory nor defeat.[12]

Far too many people remain what I call "Monday morning quarterbacks." After watching a Sunday football game, we all have opinions and pointers about what the players should have done, but we were never in the game! Many people are often tempted to critique decisions without ever stepping into leadership themselves. True leaders act, accept responsibility, and press forward in the face of opposition. To be a leader, you must step out of the judge's box and into the game.

KEY LEADERSHIP THEORIES

Several leadership theories have emerged over the years, each offering unique insights into what makes an effective leader. Following are some of the most notable theories.

- **The Trait ("Great Man") Approach** suggests that certain individuals possess innate qualities that make them natural leaders.[13]
- **The Behavioral Approach** focuses on the behaviors and actions of leaders rather than their traits or characteristics.[14]
- **The Situational Approach** emphasizes that effective leadership depends on the situation, which may require different leadership styles. Leaders must assess the situation and adapt their style accordingly.[15]
- **Transformational Leadership** emphasizes the role of leaders in inspiring and motivating followers to achieve their full potential and exceed their expectations.[16]
- **Servant Leadership** centers on the idea that leaders should prioritize serving others and meeting the needs of their followers.[17]

Each of these theories contributes to our understanding of leadership, highlighting the various aspects of being an effective leader. For the Spirit-empowered leader, the most crucial element is the active, guiding presence of the Holy Spirit.

THE HOLY SPIRIT MAKES ALL THE DIFFERENCE

The role of the Holy Spirit in leadership is paramount. He empowers leaders with wisdom, courage, and the ability to discern God's will.

Without the Spirit's presence, leadership may influence, but with His power, leadership transforms. Jesus promised His disciples, "But you will receive power when the Holy Spirit comes on you; and you will be my witnesses in Jerusalem, and in all Judea and Samaria, and to the ends of the earth" (Acts 1:8).

> *Without the Spirit's presence, leadership may influence, but with His power, leadership transforms.*

This empowerment by the Holy Spirit is essential for effective leadership, enabling leaders to fulfill their God-given mission with boldness and clarity. Scripture provides numerous examples of Spirit-empowered leadership, demonstrating how the Holy Spirit guides, convicts, empowers, and provides wisdom to leaders.

- **Moses:** In obedience and sensitivity to God's voice, Moses led the Israelites out of Egypt and through the wilderness.

- **David:** Anointed by the Holy Spirit, David led Israel with courage, humility, and strength.
- **Deborah:** A prophetess and judge, Deborah led Israel to victory by relying on God's direction.
- **Paul:** Transformed by the Holy Spirit, Paul became the most influential apostle, spreading the gospel and establishing churches throughout the Roman Empire.
- **Jesus:** The perfect leader, Jesus led with power, humility, wisdom, and sacrificial love, fulfilling God's redemptive plan for humanity.

As the greatest leader in history, Jesus embodies the perfect example of Spirit-empowered leadership. His leadership was characterized by servanthood and full obedience to God's will. In many ways Jesus redefined *leadership*, stating, "For even the Son of Man did not come to be served, but to serve, and to give his life as a ransom for many" (Mark 10:45).

Our understanding of leadership is shaped by numerous definitions, evolving viewpoints from history to the present, and foundational leadership theories that illuminate what it truly means to be a leader. Yet the distinction of the Holy Spirit in leadership allows us to lead in a way that makes a lasting impact for the glory of God in the twenty-first century.

CHAPTER 2

THE LEADERSHIP STYLES OF JESUS

As Spirit-empowered leaders, we are called to grow in wisdom, vision, and integrity, following the model of Jesus Christ—the greatest leader in human history. In this chapter we will explore key principles of leadership drawn from experience, biblical truth, and the wisdom of great leaders throughout history.

LEADERSHIP STYLES OF JESUS

There have been many outstanding leaders in human history. From Caesar Augustus to Abraham Lincoln, we can learn much about leading others effectively from historical leaders, even the wicked ones. Of anyone who has ever lived, the greatest leader was a man from Nazareth named Jesus Christ. Jesus had the most significant impact on the world and, in doing so, became our ultimate model of leadership. If we plan to discuss leadership, we must look at Jesus and the way He led during His earthly ministry. His leadership was dynamic, adapting to the needs of His mission and the people He led. Jesus demonstrated at least seven leadership styles that are worth examining if we want to become Spirit-empowered leaders.

1) Servant Leadership

Jesus redefined *leadership* by emphasizing servanthood. He told His disciples, "Anyone who wants to be first must be the very last, and the servant of all" (Mark 9:35). Later in his gospel account, Mark records Jesus' words: "For even the Son of Man did not come to be served, but to serve, and to give his life as a ransom for many" (Mark 10:45). Jesus, who has been given a name above every name and is highly exalted by the Father, saw Himself as a servant, viewing leadership in a way the world normally does not. As you will see in the following pyramid, the secular view of leadership puts the leader at the top. Even in building structures, the office of a CEO is often on the top floor. However, Jesus flipped the world's leadership pyramid by demonstrating that true leadership requires a person to move downward into greater responsibility and servanthood.

Servant leadership involves taking on the responsibility of caring for and uplifting those you are leading. Jesus exemplified this when He washed the feet of His disciples (John 13:1–17).

This act of humility and servanthood was a graphic demonstration that true leadership is not about position but about serving. A Spirit-empowered leader must be willing to serve, understanding that leadership is about serving others rather than being served.

> *A Spirit-empowered leader must be willing to serve, understanding that leadership is about serving others rather than being served.*

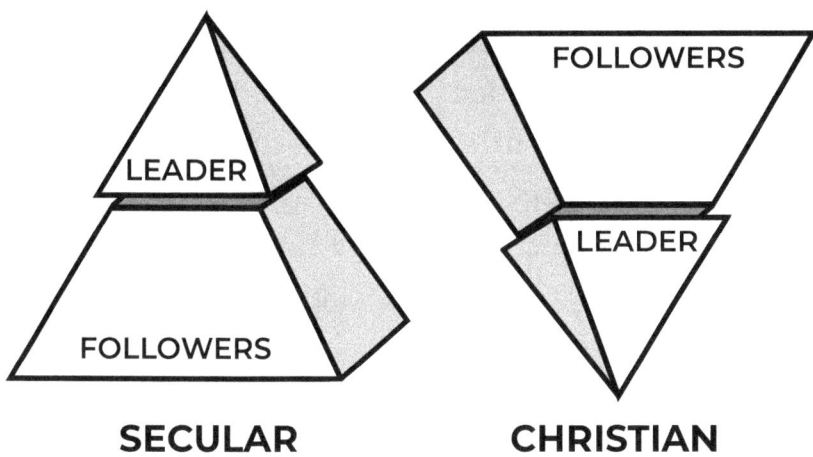

Servant leaders prioritize the well-being of those they lead. They create environments where others can thrive, encourage growth, and foster a culture of trust. Leadership always comes with some privilege, but for the Spirit-empowered leader, their life should be more about responsibility than privilege. As a Christian leader moves down the pyramid, serving more people along with more substantial responsibility, they will find that the weight of leadership increases. After all, they are at the bottom, supporting those they are called to lead.

This is why leaders must have integrity. The further you move into leadership, the heavier the pressure from increased responsibility. Without integrity, a leader will crack under this weight. We see this repeatedly in the world and even in the church. When a leader's character is unable to bear the weight of the responsibility their charisma has provided, they collapse under the weight in a variety of ways. Many of the leadership tragedies and shipwrecks we see daily in our world could be avoided if leaders saw themselves first as servants and focused on developing the integrity necessary to bear the load of leadership. Jesus, though carrying the weight of the world, remained steadfast in His mission. He did not collapse under this responsibility but led with servanthood, humility, and integrity.

2) Assertive Leadership

Though a servant, Jesus was not passive. He was firm when necessary, such as when He drove the money changers from the temple (Matthew 21:12). Servant leaders must lead with authority. Leaders must make clear decisions and follow through with them. At times, a leader must simply step forward and lead. As a leader, not everyone will agree with your choices. Leadership can be assertive while simultaneously remaining gracious and loving. Jesus gave us the ultimate example of this. Servant leaders have the organization or ministry's best interests at heart. We are called to serve others. To do this well, we will often need to be assertive and move things forward in the right direction.

3) Visionary Leadership

Jesus was a visionary leader who saw beyond the present moment. He understood the future and led His followers toward it. He declared, "Lift up your eyes, and look on the fields; for they are white already to harvest" (John 4:35, KJV). While others saw only the immediate situation, Jesus saw a world ready for transformation, and that remains how He sees the work He does among us today. He looks at us, not considering our past, but calls us into a glorious future, and He always has a great plan in mind. Leaders must also see the invisible before they can lead others toward it.

Vision is essential for leadership. Iyanla Vanzant said, "If you don't have a vision, you're going to be stuck in what you know, and the only thing you know is what you've already seen."[1] A leader without vision is simply a manager of the present, but a visionary leader sees what others cannot and inspires them to move toward a greater future. Jonathan Swift said, "Vision is the art of seeing things invisible."[2] This is particularly powerful for Spirit-empowered leaders because faith itself is about seeing the invisible and believing in what is yet to come.

> *A leader without vision is simply a manager of the present, but a visionary leader sees what others cannot and inspires them to move toward a greater future.*

Jesus always cast vision in ways that moved people to action. When He called the disciples, He not only invited them to follow Him but gave them a greater purpose: "Follow Me, and I will make you fishers of men" (Matthew 4:19, KJV). He transformed their ordinary occupations into something eternal.

Jesus' vision extended beyond His earthly ministry. He saw the global expansion of His message and commissioned His followers accordingly:

> Therefore, go and make disciples of all nations, baptizing them in the name of the Father and of the Son and of the Holy Spirit, and teaching them to obey everything I have commanded you. And surely, I am with you always, to the very end of the age.
> —MATTHEW 28:19–20

This was more than a command; it was a world-changing vision that extends to us who follow Him today. Jesus saw what was possible and empowered His followers to make it a reality.

At ORU we are currently pursuing *Impact 2030*, a visionary plan for the university's future with eight big goals. This visionary journey started when, as university president, I was alone in a mountain retreat, praying, "God, what do You want this university to look like in 2030?" He began inspiring me with thoughts and understanding about what could be possible if we worked together toward the future. I brought my "in the rough" vision back to committees and the board; we refined it and cast the vision's goals, such as reaching ten thousand students and having students from every nation represented on campus. Nothing is as exciting for a leader as watching a vision become a reality.

At Empowered21 (a kingdom initiative for the global Spirit-empowered movement) we also have a big vision: *That every person on Earth would have an authentic encounter with Jesus Christ through the power and presence of the Holy Spirit . . . by Pentecost 2033*[3]. God gave this vision to the Empowered21 Global Council in 2013 as an answer to "What is something so big that it will keep us together as a network for the long term?" God placed this vision in our hearts, and we now have initiatives in mind to move us forward with reaching every person in the world by 2033.[4]

Walt Disney, a great visionary, once said, "If you can dream it, you can do it."[5] Walt Disney passed away before the opening of Walt Disney World, but he envisioned a complex that people worldwide would visit in Central Florida. His widow and brother attended the opening parade. While standing overlooking Main Street at Disney World, Walt's brother said, "I wish Walt could have been here to see this." Immediately, Walt's widow replied, "He did see this, and that's why we're here."[6] Leaders see what others cannot. If you can dream it, you can do it!

George Lucas of *Star Wars* and *Indiana Jones* fame said, "Dreams are extremely important. You can't do it unless you can imagine it."[7] Ken Kinsey said, "You don't lead people by pointing and telling them someplace to go. You lead by going to that place and making a case."[8]

As Spirit-empowered leaders, we must ask: What is God calling us to see that others cannot? What future is He asking us to pursue? True visionary leadership is about aligning with God's purpose and leading others toward His preferred future.

4) Situational Leadership

Jesus' character, attributes, and essence are unchanging. He is "the same yesterday and today and forever" (Hebrews 13:8). Yet He adapted His leadership approach to relate to unique situations. For example, with the woman caught in adultery, Jesus stooped down, wrote in the dirt, spoke kindly to her, forgave her, did not condemn her, and instructed her to "go and sin no more" (John 8:11, NLT). Yet He confronted the Pharisees' hypocrisy and called them "whitewashed tombs" (Matthew 23:27). Effective leaders discern when to be gentle and when to be firm. They understand that leadership is not a one-size-fits-all approach.

Situational leadership requires wisdom and discernment. Leaders must be able to read the context of a situation and choose the most effective leadership response. A guiding phrase for situational leadership is "It depends." When faced with a challenge or decision, the right course of action often depends on multiple factors, including the people involved, the timing, and the specific needs of the organization.

We see an example in Moses' leadership of failing to adapt to changing circumstances. At one point God instructed him to strike a rock, and water flowed out to quench the thirst of the Israelites in the wilderness (Exodus 17:5-7). He was to be their leader for the next forty years, and God wanted the people to look to him and trust his leadership. Years later, as the people were about to enter a new season, Moses faced a similar situation. The people were about to enter Canaan, and Moses would no longer be with them. God was shifting their focus to Him as their leader and wanted the people to honor Him as holy in their eyes (Numbers 20:12). So God commanded Moses to speak to the rock. However, relying on what had worked before rather than following God's new instruction, Moses struck the rock again. Because of this act of disobedience—whether out of anger or an inability to adjust to the situation—God told Moses that he would not enter the Promised Land (Numbers 20:8-12). This serves as a powerful lesson for leaders. Leadership is dynamic, and failing to adapt to changing circumstances or fresh directions from God can hinder progress. Your leadership will evolve, requiring you to reinvent yourself multiple times to stay effective.

Leaders who practice situational leadership avoid rigid thinking. Instead, they remain flexible and responsive to the needs of their teams and the challenges they face. They do not lead based on personal preference but rather on what is required in the moment, always being obedient to God and exalting Him above themselves.

5) Submissive Leadership

The King of kings and Son of the living God modeled submission. Though all-powerful, Jesus submitted to the Father's will. "By myself, I can do nothing.... I seek not to please myself but Him who sent me" (John 5:30). Submissive leadership means acknowledging that authority comes from God and being willing to yield to His direction. We see mutual submission in the Trinity—Father, Son, and Holy Spirit submitting to one another. Jesus demonstrated ultimate submission in Gethsemane when He prayed, "Not my will, but Yours be done" (Luke 22:42). Adam's pride and disobedience brought sin into the world, and Jesus' submission to death on the cross broke sin's power. His submission was not due to weakness but from a position of divine strength and trust in the Father's plan. His example shows us one way to be a godly leader is to submit to authority.

> *Great leaders understand that submitting to godly authority brings wisdom, protection, and greater influence.*

Many people fail to realize that a leader's level of authority depends on their level of submission. You cannot expect to gain authority without being a good follower. Submissive leadership involves accountability—to mentors, boards, or governing bodies, among others. Great leaders understand that submitting to godly authority brings wisdom, protection, and greater influence. Leaders often encounter trouble when no one in their life can tell them no. God may bless, lift, and anoint them for a season, but without proper governance they can easily go off course.

Submission fosters humility. A leader who refuses to submit to authority may become prideful and unteachable. Scripture warns that "God opposes the proud but shows favor to the humble" (James 4:6). By submitting to authority, we gain authority; by resisting, we forfeit it. Through modeling submission, leaders inspire those they lead to walk in humility, integrity, and faithfulness.

6) Leadership Through Weakness

Jesus, though not weak, led through weakness and vulnerability. I have always been amazed that the Son of God and Master of the universe asked His disciples for help. In the Garden of Gethsemane, He asked His disciples to stay awake and pray with Him (Matthew 26:36–41). Though ultimately they fell asleep, Jesus knew He was empowering them, drawing them to Himself, and making them feel needed when He asked for their assistance. Jesus understood that leading out of weakness, vulnerably, and asking for help draws followers to one's leadership.

Unlike Jesus, we are flawed and need help. Leaders who acknowledge their weaknesses and seek assistance build stronger teams. Instead of presenting an image of self-sufficiency, great leaders involve others in the mission and value their contributions. True strength comes from recognizing that we cannot accomplish great things alone. We need a team. If you are not transparent enough to acknowledge your need for help, you will not be a good leader. Soliciting help is not a weakness; strength and vulnerability are required for effective leadership.

I have often discovered the power of asking for help. Having others help me empowers me, but they are also empowered by having someone in authority ask for their assistance. This is a powerful tool for every leader. Invariably, when I ask people to help me, they feel respected, honored, treasured, valued, and seen. Consequently, I can gain the expertise of others to overcome my areas of weakness. I would have failed multiple times in my leadership if I had not been willing to ask for help from those I am leading. Actually, I have failed many times, but I would have failed even more. Jesus led the way in this as the Son of God, though He needed nothing from anyone. He empowered His followers by asking for their help.

7) Principled Leadership

Though Jesus responded differently to different groups and at various times, He remained steadfast in who He is. His core values and life principles never changed:

1) **Truth**—Jesus declared, "I am the way and the truth and the life" (John 14:6). He embodied and spoke truth and expected His followers to do the same.
2) **Love, Respect, and Honor**—Even when rebuking them, Jesus cared for people. We feel this in our relationship

with Him. He loves us deeply as He leads us through life, and even when He chastens us, we feel His love.
3) **Integrity**—Jesus never compromised. He was crucified for claiming to be the Son of God, not because of a moral failure.
4) **Humility**—Jesus was strong yet gentle. He was humble and served all.
5) **Character**—Jesus never wavered in who He is.

Jesus was trustworthy, and leadership is built on trust. If a leader lacks integrity, they will eventually lose credibility. Leadership travels on the currency of trust—if people cannot trust you, they will not follow you. A principled leader operates with strong values, refuses to compromise, and leads with character. A leader who compromises truth for convenience, power, or personal gain will ultimately fail. As John Maxwell said, "You build trust each time you choose integrity over image, truth over convenience, honor over personal gain."[9] Many leaders possess charisma, a great personality, energy, and likability, but without character they collapse. Their character has not developed to match the level of their charisma.

Spirit-empowered leadership follows Jesus' example of servant leadership, assertive leadership, visionary leadership, situational leadership, submissive leadership, leadership through weakness, and principled leadership. Will you commit to following Jesus' example of leading with wisdom, integrity, and the power of the Holy Spirit in your world?

CHAPTER 3

LEADING BY THE SPIRIT

FLESH VS. SPIRIT

The greatest challenge in your Christian life and leadership will not be opposition from others but the war between your flesh and the Spirit. The good news is that God has not left us to fight this battle in our own strength.

God's Word is sharper than a double-edged sword (Hebrews 4:12), and as we engage with Scripture, it cuts deeply within us, helping us discern our thoughts and attitudes. Scripture contrasts the works of the flesh with the fruit of the Spirit. This distinction is crucial for those who seek to be

Spirit-empowered leaders. Paul addresses this struggle in his letters to the Romans and Galatians:

> Those who live according to the flesh have their minds set on what the flesh desires; but those who live in accordance with the Spirit have their minds set on what the Spirit desires. The mind governed by the flesh is death, but the mind governed by the Spirit is life and peace. The mind governed by the flesh is hostile to God; it does not submit to God's law, nor can it do so. Those who are in the realm of the flesh cannot please God.
> —Romans 8:5–9

> So I say, walk by the Spirit, and you will not gratify the desires of the flesh. For the flesh desires what is contrary to the Spirit, and the Spirit what is contrary to the flesh. They are in conflict with each other, so that you are not to do whatever you want. But if you are led by the Spirit, you are not under the law.
> —Galatians 5:16–18

Paul explains that if we walk by the Spirit, we will not fulfill the desires of the flesh. Everyone experiences this tension—the struggle between the flesh and the Spirit. The only way to become Spirit-empowered leaders is by learning to win this battle. The law alone cannot give us the strength to please God or live in the Spirit. Only the Holy Spirit can empower us to overcome the works of the flesh.

THE WORKS OF THE FLESH

Whenever I face a new health challenge, one of the first places I turn to is the internet. Yes, I tend to search the medical websites first and see what they say about my symptoms. I know I should consult a physician first, but the websites give me an overview of what the symptoms I am experiencing could indicate. Of course, after I finish reading the lists, I feel sicker than before and end up at the doctor's office after all.

In Galatians, Paul provides a list of symptoms of living after the flesh. In other words, he shares some of the manifestations of what fleshly living will produce so that we can examine ourselves. He also provides a sober warning: "Those who live like this will not inherit the kingdom of God" (Galatians 5:21). If we are to take this seriously, we must examine the list Paul gives us and ask, "Am I living according to the flesh?" Like a symptom checklist, Paul offers us an overview of ways the flesh manifests.

The word *flesh* comes from the Greek word *sarx*, meaning "human nature" or "carnality." It refers to the lower, base part of humanity—our fallen nature that gravitates toward sin. To live carnally is to prioritize pleasing the flesh over pleasing God.

During my many years of ministry, I have rarely heard anyone take Paul's list apart and truly identify what he means by these symptoms. Similarly, engaging with a spiritual health journal and understanding biblical terminology will help us recognize if our problem is living according to our fleshly desires. By becoming familiar with the meaning of each term, we are better equipped to acknowledge their presence in our lives, just as accurately reading a doctor's report helps us diagnose and address physical ailments. This honest self-assessment is not meant for condemnation but for clarity and transformation, so that, empowered by the Spirit, we may pursue healing and wholeness.

Paul's symptom list for living after the flesh includes:

1) **Sexual Immorality**—The word Paul uses for sexual immorality comes from the Greek word *porneia*. This includes adultery, fornication, and the use of pornography. God designed sex as a beautiful gift within marriage, but when misused, it pulls us away from God and walking in the Spirit.
2) **Impurity**—Embracing unclean thoughts, language, and relationships, and enjoying inappropriate jokes or entertaining unwholesome thoughts indicates impurity in one's life.
3) **Debauchery**—Overindulgence in life's pleasures and making pleasure our primary pursuit rather than God is debauchery.
4) **Idolatry**—Worshipping anything other than God is idolatry. This includes looking to something or someone else for comfort, stability, or guidance in place of Him.
5) **Witchcraft**—Seeking supernatural power apart from God through spells, incantations, sorcery, or even the use of drugs is witchcraft. These are all designed to empower

the participants with power beyond themselves. Scripture also likens rebellion to witchcraft (1 Samuel 15:23). Rebellion is an attempt to empower oneself against authority.

6) **Hatred**—Malicious or unjustifiable feelings toward others is hatred, and it can also involve a desire to destroy or hurt another. Scripture teaches that "anyone who hates a brother or sister is a murderer, and you know that no murderer has eternal life residing in him" (1 John 3:15).

7) **Discord**—Disharmony, contention, quarrels, or strife; deliberately inciting conflict and disagreement instead of seeking peace promotes discord.

8) **Jealousy**—Jealousy is translated from the Greek word *zēlos* and refers to a possessive, burning desire to have something. It is driven by covetousness rather than contentment.

9) **Fits of Rage**—Temper tantrums and acting out one's anger are fits of rage.

10) **Selfish Ambition**—Assertion for personal gain at the expense of others, rather than seeking God's glory, is selfish ambition.

11) **Dissensions**—Insurrection, sedition, fighting against authority, or standing in opposition to those ordained by God to lead are dissensions, as is rebelling against authority and sowing seeds of division.

12) **Factions**—Rivalry and self-seeking to win followers cause factions. If you put together the words *strife* and *hireling*, you have faction. Faction creates division for personal gain.

13) **Envy**—The feeling of displeasure about others' prosperity, blessings, or advantage is envy. It is different from jealousy in that envy desires to deprive another of what he or she has rather than just possessing it for oneself.
14) **Drunkenness**—Intoxication, inebriation, or numbing oneself with alcohol or substances rather than turning to God for comfort describes drunkenness.
15) **Orgies**—Partying, reveling out of control, and indulging with others are orgies.

Paul concludes with a strong warning:

> Do not be deceived: God cannot be mocked. A man reaps what he sows. Whoever sows to please their flesh, from the flesh will reap destruction; whoever sows to please the Spirit, from the Spirit will reap eternal life.
> —GALATIANS 6:7–8

To overcome the flesh, we must strengthen our relationship with the Holy Spirit. Feeding the flesh leads to destruction, but feeding the Spirit leads to life. The choice is ours. Which will we feed?

An old story paints this picture well. It is about a man who owned two dogs, a black one and a white one. The two dogs were always fighting. Someone asked him, "Which one usually wins?" He replied, "Whichever one I feed the most." This principle can be applied to our walk with God. If you feed the flesh, it will dominate. If you feed the Spirit, you will overcome the flesh and walk in victory.

THE FRUIT OF THE SPIRIT: CHARACTERISTICS OF A SPIRIT-EMPOWERED LEADER

The other side of the sword of God's Word is the fruit of the Spirit. If we walk in the Spirit and do not satisfy the desires of the flesh, the Holy Spirit will produce good fruit in our lives. Both the works of the flesh and the fruit of the Spirit serve as a dashboard to gauge how we are living. If the works of the flesh list reveals symptoms of a heart overwhelmed by the flesh, then Paul's list of the fruit of the Spirit could serve as a checklist for healthy spirituality. If we walk according to and live in the Spirit, then fruit will naturally be produced in our lives. This fruit shows us that God is at work in us and that we are walking with Him. Paul's list of the fruit of the Spirit is also found in Galatians.

> But the fruit of the Spirit is love, joy, peace, forbearance, kindness, goodness, faithfulness, gentleness and self-control. Against such things there is no law. Those who belong to Christ Jesus have crucified the flesh with its passions and desires. Since we live by the Spirit, let us keep in step with the Spirit.
> —Galatians 5:22–25

ONE FRUIT, NINE EXPRESSIONS

The original Greek of the text reveals that Paul refers to the fruit of the Spirit as a singular "fruit" and not "fruits." These nine expressions are part of a whole. An orange is a great example of this. In almost every instance when I open an orange to demonstrate the fruit of the Spirit concept, it will have nine pieces (only once in the last ten years has this not been true). Just as the orange is one fruit with multiple segments inside, the fruit of the Spirit is one singular fruit with nine unique expressions: love, joy, peace, forbearance (patience), kindness, goodness, faithfulness, gentleness, and self-control. These characteristics are connected and grow together as we abide in Christ and walk in the Spirit.

Just as a tree is recognized by its fruit, so is a Christian. If you go to an apple tree, you expect apples. You would be shocked to see plums or any other kind of fruit. An apple tree produces only apples. In the same way, if you observe the life of a Christian, you expect to find Christlike qualities.

THIS FRUIT OF THE SPIRIT REPRESENTS THE PERSONALITY OF JESUS.

If you could have interviewed Jesus' disciples during His earthly ministry, they would have told you, "He is loving, full of joy, peaceful, patient, kind, good, faithful, gentle, and self-controlled." That is just who He is! Jesus embodied the fruit of the Holy Spirit.

After Jesus' death and resurrection, He ascended into heaven, leaving His followers as representatives of Himself on earth. As followers of Christ, we are to reflect His nature to the world, and this happens through His fruit in our lives.

How do we do this? How do we produce spiritual fruit in our lives and consistently point the world to Jesus, showing them what He is like? John records Jesus' teaching that fruitfulness comes from abiding in Him. "I am the vine; you are the branches. If you remain in me and I in you, you will bear much fruit; apart from me, you can do nothing" (John 15:5).

Jesus frequently used vineyard imagery in His ministry because His listeners were familiar with the grape-growing process as part of their culture. A grapevine is deeply rooted, and its branches spread far from the root, producing clusters of grapes. The vine provides the necessary nourishment, and the branches must remain connected to the vine if they are to thrive. When we, as branches, abide or remain in Christ, the vine, we receive the spiritual nutrients needed to bear fruit. When a branch is disconnected, it withers and becomes fruitless.

As a vineyard requires careful pruning to maximize its yield, God refines us so that we become even more fruitful. This is not always a pleasant process in the moment, but it is necessary to live in the fullness of Christlikeness. He may allow certain circumstances in our lives, send people along our path, or teach us important lessons to act as an agent in the process of pruning us so we can become more like Him.

A branch does not bear fruit by striving—it simply remains connected to the vine. We cannot produce good fruit in our lives by sheer willpower. Through more than fifty years of walking with Jesus, this has been a learning process for me. I've experienced frustration at times when I need more joy in my life, and I try to have joy. If I find I need to be kinder and gentler, I strive to be so in my efforts. My attempts at demonstrating fruit never work. The more I focus on trying to produce fruit, the less successful I seem to be. I have learned that the way to fruitfulness is in an intimate relationship with the source, Jesus Christ. When I remain in Him and my relationship with Him is strong, then spiritual fruit grows. A sure sign that we need to reconnect with Jesus is when we do not see good fruit in our lives.

> *A branch does not bear fruit by striving—it simply remains connected to the vine.*

Spiritual fruit is also a gauge of spiritual maturity. Like natural fruit, we need time to grow in spiritual fruitfulness. A young tree does not bear fruit immediately. It can take years for a plant or tree to produce fruit that is ripe and ready to eat. Christian maturity is a process of growing in Christ. Spiritual fruit is the result of spiritual maturity, and when we fail to see the fruit of the Spirit in our lives, our growth has been stunted in some way. Henry Drummond said, "No one can get joy by merely asking for it. It is one of the ripest fruits of the Christian life, and, like all fruits, must be grown."[1]

THE GREATEST OF THESE IS LOVE

While all nine expressions of spiritual fruit flow from the Holy Spirit, love is both the foundation and the capstone of the fruit of the Spirit. Love is like an orange peel encasement holding the nine pieces of fruit, and it is also one of the pieces. We would have difficulty overstating the power of love in the believer's life and the fact that love is indeed the greatest sign of spiritual maturity for any disciple. The Greek language distinguishes between different types of love: *érōs* (romantic love), *phileó* (brotherly love), and *agapé* (selfless, divine love). The fruit of the Spirit is rooted in *agapé*—God's unconditional love flowing through us. Paul emphasized that faith, hope, and love remain, but the greatest of these is love (1 Corinthians 13:13).

When I was five years old, my dad left our home. Ultimately, he and my mother divorced, so I grew up with my mom and my grandparents.[2] My grandparents, Mammy and Pop, built an addition to their home to provide space for my mom, two sisters, and me. In my corner bedroom, I remember having a plaque on my wall that read "Love never fails." I would see that small plaque every morning when I got out of bed, and it was the last thing I saw every night before going to sleep. Years later my father recommitted his life to the Lord and eventually reconciled with my mom and our family. We saw a miraculous example of God's grace and love in my parents' lives. When Dad and I renewed our relationship, one of the many important lessons he taught me was, "Billy, if love doesn't work, don't try anything else." Over the years, he repeatedly reminded me of this principle. Many of Dad's friends still recall this statement, and it has had a deep impact on my life. In every leadership position I have held, I have been reminded of the power of love and the truth that if love doesn't work, I should not try anything else. We must lead with love. The plaque on my bedroom wall and God's Word remain true: love never fails.

As Spirit-empowered leaders, we are called to embody the fruit of the Spirit. People should experience the character of Christ through us. In many ways, the presence of spiritual fruit in our lives will determine the effectiveness of our leadership. A Spirit-empowered leader does not merely operate out of power or earthly authority but leads with character, displaying the personality of Jesus to the world.

> *A Spirit-empowered leader does not merely operate out of power or earthly authority but leads with character, displaying the personality of Jesus to the world.*

The more we focus on and develop our relationship with Christ, the more His nature will shine through us, drawing others into His presence and transforming our lives. Recently, I experienced this when I had the honor of praying with the First Lady of the United States, Melania Trump. We conducted an interview together regarding her Fostering the Future initiative, which helps young men and women who have aged out of foster care to obtain a college education.[3] She has established a scholarship to help with this, and ORU is one of the institutions where former foster children have benefited. Before the interview, I asked if it would be possible to conclude with a prayer. Her team granted my request, and when I finished praying, Melania said, "That was beautiful; I felt the Holy Spirit." This was an amazing moment for me to see how God's evident presence touched the First Lady of the United States through me. Wherever I go, I want people to experience the goodness, the presence, and the love of Jesus. This can only happen if I have a deep relationship with Jesus Christ.

When you are in a true relationship with Jesus, not only do you have the promise of eternal life in heaven, but you have the pleasure of displaying Him to the world so they can also experience Him. The fruit of the Spirit is the outward evidence of an inward transformation. It is the personality of Jesus growing in us and manifesting through us. Jesus designed our lives in such a way that we need Him. He wants a relationship with each one of us. If we remain in Christ, yield to the Holy Spirit, and cultivate intimacy with Him, we will naturally bear much fruit. This is the true measure of spiritual maturity and a key to Spirit-empowered leadership.

CHAPTER 4

LEADERSHIP AND THE GIFTS OF THE SPIRIT

While the fruit of the Spirit reflects the personality of Jesus, the gifts of the Spirit show His abilities. If the disciples who walked with Jesus were interviewed and we asked what He was like personally, they would likely mention the qualities of the fruit of the Spirit. However, if we asked them to describe what Jesus could do, they would probably use terms associated with the gifts of the Spirit. When discussing spiritual gifts and how Jesus' abilities are demonstrated or evident through us, we must remember that fruit, not gifts, indicates spiritual maturity. During the apostle Paul's ministry, the church in Corinth demonstrated this well. Many believers exhibited spiritual gifts but lacked maturity, which is evidenced by the fruit of the Spirit. Paul emphasized that without love—the first and greatest fruit of the Spirit—all other manifestations of the Spirit are meaningless.

> If I speak in the tongues of men or of angels, but do not have love, I am only a resounding gong or a clanging cymbal. If I have the gift of prophecy and can fathom all mysteries and all knowledge, and if I have a faith that can move mountains, but do not have love, I am nothing. If I give all I possess to the poor and give over my body to hardship that I may boast, but do not have love, I gain nothing. Love is patient, love is kind. It does not envy, it does not boast, it is not proud. It does not dishonor others, it is not self-seeking, it is not easily angered, it keeps no record of wrongs. Love does not delight in evil but rejoices with the truth. It always protects, always trusts, always hopes, always perseveres. Love never fails.
> —1 CORINTHIANS 13:1–8

> *The gifts of the Spirit demonstrate the power and abilities of Jesus through us to the world.*

The presence of spiritual gifts does not necessarily indicate maturity—spiritual fruit does. As a leader, you may experience frustration seeing God use people in the gifts of the Spirit, while noticing they are not very mature. Understanding that the fruit and gifts are different is crucial. Maturity is demonstrated through good fruit.

The gifts of the Spirit demonstrate the power and abilities of Jesus through us to the world. These gifts are supernatural empowerment given by the Holy Spirit to equip believers for service, to edify the church, and to testify to the power of God. Paul expresses this in his letter to the Romans: "I long to see you so that I may impart to you some spiritual gift to make you strong" (Romans 1:11). The gifts of the Spirit strengthen believers and equip leaders to represent Jesus effectively. Unlike the fruit of the Spirit, the gifts are not a mark of spiritual maturity. God uses whom He pleases when He pleases to operate in the gifts. Paul urges believers to passionately and earnestly desire spiritual gifts. Operating in the gifts of the Spirit is an essential part of being a Spirit-empowered leader.

PRINCIPLES OF ALL THE GIFTS OF THE HOLY SPIRIT

Before exploring the specific gifts, we must understand key principles about their operation so we can properly steward what God gives us as we lead.

1) *The gifts of the Spirit are to glorify Jesus.* They are not to elevate the person through whom they are functioning. When the gifts are operational in us, people should walk

away saying, "Wow, Jesus is amazing," rather than, "Wow, you are amazing."

2) *The gifts of the Spirit are to edify the body of Christ.* Paul tells us that spiritual gifts are meant to edify the church: "Now to each one the manifestation of the Spirit is given for the common good" (1 Corinthians 12:7). When spiritual gifts are flowing, they supernaturally charge the church. They are not for personal gain but to bless others and point them to Jesus.

3) *The gifts of the Spirit are God-given.* Spiritual gifts cannot be earned, bought, or manipulated. In Samaria, Simon the sorcerer tried to buy the power of the Holy Spirit, only to be rebuked by Peter: "May your money perish with you, because you thought you could buy the gift of God with money!" (Acts 8:20). The gifts are not something we can conjure or invoke; they are divine gifts that come in God's timing and way.

4) *The gifts of the Spirit are not for self-boasting or self-exaltation.* While God gives these gifts freely, they must be exercised in faith, humility, and alignment with His purposes. A gift that is misused or disconnected from love is ineffective (1 Corinthians 13). This relates to the first principle that the gifts are to glorify the Lord. The gifts must flow from hearts of love, or they lose their impact.

The New Testament provides three major lists of spiritual gifts, found in Ephesians 4, Romans 12, and 1 Corinthians 12.

I will address the gifts in categories that I have created so that you can understand the differences between them.

THE MINISTRY GIFTS (EPHESIANS 4)

Paul describes five ministry gifts that Christ gave to equip believers. These are ministries through gifted individuals within the body of Christ that God uses for governance and the work of the church.

> So Christ himself gave the apostles, the prophets, the evangelists, the pastors and teachers, to equip his people for works of service, so that the body of Christ may be built up until we all reach unity in the faith and in the knowledge of the Son of God and become mature, attaining to the whole measure of the fullness of Christ.
> —Ephesians 4:11–13

Some have identified these as the fivefold ministry gifts:

1) **Apostles**—They govern and bring cohesiveness to the church. Often the people operating in this ministry are leaders of networks, ministries, organizations, denominations, and other arenas. Apostles help move the church cohesively forward. The office of the apostle can often be

misunderstood. I believe that we witness two levels to this gifting. The first level of apostle is those who personally walked with Jesus during His earthly ministry. They had a unique ministry, and many of them were used to author the New Testament. Yet the gift of apostleship did not die with John, the last of the original twelve to pass into eternity. Rather, it continues today on a secondary level. Scripture indicates that some were called apostles in early Christianity who were not among the original twelve. People such as Silas and Timothy (1 Thessalonians 1:1; 2:6), Andronicus and Junia (Romans 16:7), and Barnabas (Acts 14:14), among others, are called apostles, although they were not among the original twelve. They were functional apostles serving as part of the foundation of the church. This foundational role continues today with those gifted as apostles to the church.

2) **Prophets**—They guide, declaring God's Word and bringing His direction to the church. The words that prophets prophesy are often used by God in critical moments when clarity is needed.
3) **Evangelists**—They seek and gather the lost. Evangelists bring new people into the body of Christ by proclaiming the gospel.
4) **Pastors**—A pastor guards and oversees the church. Pastors are shepherds who nurture, care for, love, and protect the flock and their congregations.
5) **Teachers**—This ministry gift grounds believers in biblical truth. After the Holy Spirit works in a person's heart, God

uses teachers to connect the believer's head with their heart by imparting knowledge and helping them gain biblical literacy.

A helpful analogy I use to remember and teach the five ministry gifts is an illustration of a hand, comparing each finger to a specific role.

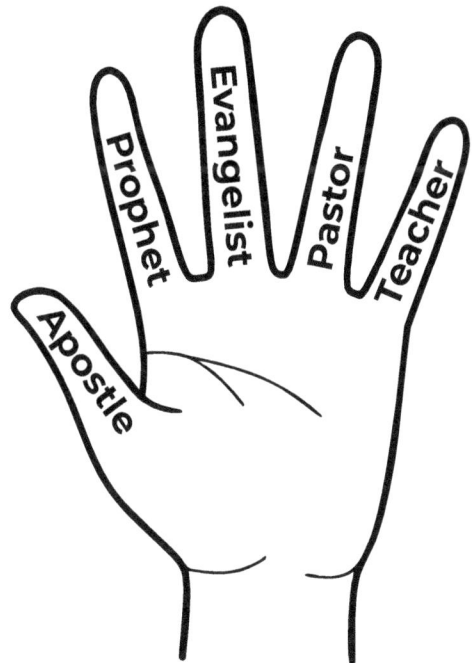

1) **Thumb (Apostle):** Just as the thumb is critical to the hand and helps you grasp objects, the apostle holds things together and provides stability.
2) **Index Finger (Prophet):** The index finger is used to point just as a prophet is used by God to point the way, bringing divine revelation that shows the church which way to go.

3) **Middle Finger (Evangelist):** The middle finger is the longest on the hand, representing an evangelist reaching beyond others, looking for the lost, and bringing them into the fold.
4) **Ring Finger (Pastor):** The ring finger represents the pastor because in many ways a pastor is married to the church. They consistently bring care to the people of God.
5) **Pinkie (Teacher):** The smallest finger on your hand can reach inside the ear canal in the same way a teacher can get inside your head with teaching and understanding.

Often these five ministry gifts intertwine, and an apostle will function in all these gifts throughout their ministry, as seen in the case of the apostle Paul. We see examples in the New Testament of Paul being used as an apostle, a prophet, an evangelist, a pastor, and a teacher. When I first began in ministry, I started as an evangelist. I traveled, telling the good news of Jesus. As I did, God would also use me prophetically to speak into people's lives. I continue to operate in these gifts, but over time I've also developed an apostolic oversight ministry. When I first became president of ORU, I had to operate in several of these roles simultaneously. Throughout my journey I have found myself serving in various roles within the body of Christ, both locally and globally. At times, I have functioned as a prophet, an evangelist, a pastor, or a teacher, depending on where God has called me to serve.

Your faith community will help you understand if you are gifted in these areas. When I was a young man and felt God was leading me into ministry, I submitted to my local church. They tested my calling by having me preach and serve in different areas. They then confirmed that yes, God was calling me to operate in ministry gifts. Your faith community can do this for you.

THE GRACE GIFTS (ROMANS 12)

In his letter to the Romans, Paul lists what are often called "grace gifts," as they reflect God's gracious empowerment in a believer's life.

> For by the grace given me I say to every one of you: Do not think of yourself more highly than you ought, but rather think of yourself with sober judgment, in accordance with the faith God has distributed to each of you. For just as each of us has one body with many members, and these members do not all have the same function, so in Christ we, though many, form one body, and each member belongs to all the others. We have different gifts, according to the grace given to each of us. If your gift is prophesying, then prophesy in accordance with your faith; if it is serving, then serve; if it is teaching, then teach; if it is to encourage, then give encouragement; if it is giving, then give generously; if it is to lead, do it diligently; if it is to show mercy, do it cheerfully.
>
> —ROMANS 12:3–8

I do not believe this is an exhaustive list, but rather, Paul is giving us examples of how God's grace may bestow gifts in our lives. In contrast to ministry gifts, grace gifts tend to be revealed in us as natural abilities from birth. While supernaturally given by God, they appear as an ongoing giftedness in one's life.

Paul's list includes:

- Prophecy
- Serving (Hospitality)
- Teaching
- Exhortation
- Giving
- Leadership or Administration
- Mercy

Interestingly, leadership or administration is included in this list. As previously mentioned, leaders are both born and made. This is biblical. Leadership can be developed, but sometimes leadership emerges naturally in a person, even a child. If you were to observe a nursery, you would find certain children acting as leaders. They will organize games, help other children stand in line, and lead their friends. They have a natural giftedness for leadership.

Further demonstrating the nature of the grace gifts, consider someone with the gift of hospitality. People with this gift tend to make sure everybody's comfortable. During a party they ensure everybody has cake. As children, they are the ones who organize the tea party. If someone has this gifting, they tend to be gifted in hospitality, even if they are not following Christ. You can be in a bar and notice someone who has the gift of hospitality. They make sure everybody's comfortable and has a good seat, their coats are hung up, and they all have the right drinks. Why is that? I believe that when they were conceived, God imparted and assigned this gift to them. Unlike other groups of spiritual gifts, grace gifts can often be displayed throughout a person's life. Then, when the individual is converted to Christ, God uses this gift to point people to Jesus.

SUPERNATURAL GIFTS (1 CORINTHIANS 12)

I identify the gifts that Paul wrote about to the Corinthians as supernatural gifts. These gifts tend not to be resident like grace gifts. They appear in an instant when God uses someone supernaturally, and He does not always use the same person in the same way each time.

> Now about the gifts of the Spirit, brothers and sisters, I do not want you to be uninformed. You know that when you were pagans, somehow or other you were influenced and led astray to mute idols. Therefore, I want you to know that no one who is speaking by the Spirit of God says, "Jesus be cursed," and no one can say, "Jesus is Lord," except by the Holy Spirit. There are different kinds of gifts, but the same Spirit distributes

them. There are different kinds of service, but the same Lord. There are different kinds of working, but in all of them and in everyone it is the same God at work. Now to each one the manifestation of the Spirit is given for the common good. To one there is given through the Spirit a message of wisdom, to another a message of knowledge by means of the same Spirit, to another faith by the same Spirit, to another gifts of healing by that one Spirit, to another miraculous powers, to another prophecy, to another distinguishing between spirits, to another speaking in different kinds of tongues, and to still another the interpretation of tongues. All these are the work of one and the same Spirit, and he distributes them to each one, just as he determines.

—1 Corinthians 12:1–11

Supernatural gifts can be grouped into three categories:

1) REVELATION GIFTS

These gifts impart an understanding that one could not know without it supernaturally being revealed.

A message of wisdom is divine insight for complex situations.

God is all-wise and omniscient. When God uses a person in this way, He does not give them all His wisdom. No human could handle that! Rather, God reveals pieces of wisdom in the inspiration of the moment. It is important that all of us as believers possess and seek wisdom, as God's Word says, "If any of you lacks wisdom, you should ask God, who gives generously to all without finding fault, and it will be given to you" (James 1:5). However, a message of wisdom is a supernatural infusion of understanding that you would not have on your own to be used by God in a moment to demonstrate the supernatural wisdom of Jesus.

We see this gift in action in a meeting of the early church. James says, "It is my judgment, therefore, that we should not make it difficult for the gentiles who are turning to God. Instead, we should write to them, telling them to abstain from food polluted by idols, from sexual immorality, from the meat of strangled animals, and from blood" (Acts 15:19–20). The church was in the middle of a challenging controversy. They were discussing whether they should require gentiles to submit to the physical sign of the Jewish covenant of circumcision after receiving salvation. They convened a council in Jerusalem to resolve this matter, and two opposing sides were present. The Judaizers wanted the Christian gentiles to come under the sign of the covenant as a necessary next step. The gentiles felt that being saved was enough and they should not have to go through this physical pain. The two sides could not agree until James received a message of wisdom from the Holy Spirit. Through this supernatural insight God settled the issue. The church experienced peace and moved forward in unity.

A message of knowledge is supernatural knowledge about a person or situation.

This is demonstrated in the Ananias and Sapphira narrative. The couple sold a piece of property and decided they would give a portion of the money to the apostles. They had previously witnessed when Barnabas did this, and he was given a position of favor (Acts 4:36–37). They too wanted special favor; however, they wanted to keep some of the money for themselves. When they brought the money to the apostles, Peter asked if it was the full price of the land. Ananias could have told the truth and would have been fine. God did not require them to give the entire income from the land. Instead, Ananias chose to lie, stating that this was the full price. In a moment of supernatural inspiration, Peter received a message of knowledge: "Didn't it belong to you before it was sold? And after it was sold, wasn't the money at your disposal? What made you think of doing such a thing? You have not lied just to human beings but to God" (Acts 5:4).

Peter could have only known this information through revelation from the Holy Spirit. Look at what happened next: "When Ananias heard this, he fell down and died. And great fear seized all who heard what had happened. Then some young men came forward, wrapped up his body, and carried him out and buried him" (Acts 5:5–6).

After Ananias died, Sapphira approached the apostles, not knowing what had happened to her husband. She also lied and suffered the same fate:

About three hours later, his wife came in, not knowing what had happened. Peter asked her, "Tell me, is this the price you and Ananias got for the land?" "Yes," she said, "that is the price." Peter said to her, "How could you conspire to test the Spirit of the Lord? Listen! The feet of the men who buried your husband are at the door, and they will carry you out also." At that moment, she fell down at his feet and died. Then the young men came in and, finding her dead, carried her out and buried her beside her husband. Great fear seized the whole church and all who heard about these events.
—ACTS 5:7–11

Some people read this chapter and say Peter killed Ananias and Sapphira, but this is not the case. Rather, Peter had a word or message of knowledge revealing what they were saying was not true. The couple would have been fine if they had only told the truth, but Peter received a revelation that they were lying to the Holy Spirit.

God has all knowledge. When you function with this gift, God does not impart all His knowledge to you. Your head might explode if He did! Instead, the Holy Spirit gives you a portion of God's knowledge for the moment. We should all pursue greater knowledge and study to show ourselves approved (2 Timothy 2:15), but this gift is supernatural. You receive knowledge you could not have obtained on your own but only from God, imparting it to you instantly and supernaturally.

Operating in the gifts of words of wisdom and words of knowledge is vital in leadership. When you are full of the Holy Spirit and invite Him into your leadership, He will use you in supernatural ways to bless others.

> *When you are full of the Holy Spirit and invite Him into your leadership, He will use you in supernatural ways to bless others.*

Discerning of Spirits

This is the ability to understand the spirit at work in a life or situation. This gift is vital because we live in a world where many different spiritual influences are constantly at work around us. "For we wrestle not against flesh and blood, but against principalities, against powers, against the rulers of the darkness of this world, against spiritual wickedness in high places" (Ephesians 6:12, KJV).

One example of this gift of discerning spirits is given when Paul and Silas were ministering in Philippi. The writer Luke shares their experience:

> Once when we were going to the place of prayer, we were met by a female slave who had a spirit by which she predicted the future. She earned a great deal of money for her owners by fortune-telling. She followed Paul and

the rest of us, shouting, "These men are servants of the Most High God, who are telling you the way to be saved."
—ACTS 16:16–17

What this woman was saying was absolutely true. These men were servants of God who were proclaiming the way of salvation. The problem was not what she was saying but the spirit with which she said it. "Finally Paul became so annoyed that he turned around and said to the spirit, 'In the name of Jesus Christ I command you to come out of her!' At that moment, the spirit left her" (Acts 16:18).

Sometimes I meet Christians who say, "That person just gives me a weird feeling." This is not necessarily the gift of discerning spirits. However, with this gift you may often see through something that looks good but discern that behind it is an ungodly spirit at work. As a leader, you must be able to discern the spirit behind what is happening.

2) POWER GIFTS

These gifts display supernatural power through the believer to show the world what Jesus can do.

Faith is supernatural confidence in God's ability.

Paul demonstrated this gift when he was in Lystra.

> In Lystra there sat a man who was lame. He had been that way from birth and had never walked. He listened

to Paul as he was speaking. Paul looked directly at him, saw that he had faith to be healed and called out, "Stand up on your feet!" At that, the man jumped up and began to walk.

—ACTS 14:8–10

We are not told that Paul prayed for, laid his hands on, or cried out to God for the cripple in Lystra. Instead, he suddenly received supernatural faith and declared, "Get up and walk." This is supernatural faith—the kind of faith Jesus had when He said to the storm, "Be still," and it stopped (Mark 4:39). This kind of faith moves mountains and witnesses miracles. I've experienced this a few times over the years. I stopped merely praying for people and declared instead, "You are healed," and they were healed. We should all have faith, but the gift of faith is supernatural.

Healing is a miraculous restoration of health.

Multiple kinds of healing are experienced, but let's explore one instance.

> There was an estate nearby that belonged to Publius, the chief official of the island. He welcomed us to his home and showed us generous hospitality for three days. His father was sick in bed, suffering from fever and dysentery. Paul went in to see him and, after prayer, placed his hands on him and healed him.

> When this had happened, the rest of the sick on the island came and were cured.
>
> —ACTS 28:7–9

Paul was shipwrecked on the island of Malta. As a prisoner, he endured severe cold, wind, and rain when his boat crashed on the island. After Paul was bitten by a serpent but not harmed, the people of the island brought those who were sick to Paul, and he healed them. This is a demonstration of the gifts of healing, which is different from being healed personally. This is when God uses you to heal someone else. He may use you to bring healing to people who are hurting mentally, emotionally, financially, relationally, or physically.

Miraculous powers are signs and wonders beyond natural explanation.

This gift is not receiving a miracle but God working a miracle through you. "Everyone was filled with awe at the many wonders and signs performed by the apostles" (Acts 2:43). God used the apostles in wonders and signs. Luke records one miracle when a woman had died and Peter raised her from the dead.

> Peter sent them all out of the room; then he got down on his knees and prayed. Turning toward the dead woman, he said, "Tabitha, get up." She opened her eyes, and seeing Peter she sat up. He took her by the hand and helped her to her feet. Then he called for

the believers, especially the widows, and presented her to them alive.

—ACTS 9:40–41

Peter demonstrated what Jesus can do—raise the dead!

3) PROCLAMATION GIFTS

These gifts involve speaking a word from God clearly and faithfully to communicate the message that people most need to hear.

Prophecy is speaking forth God's message.

Prophecy can be either foretelling or forthtelling, meaning one can either predict the future or exhort. This supernatural gift differs from typical preaching. Most preaching has an element of prophecy, but the gift of prophecy is beyond normal. When the prophet Joel said, "Your sons and your daughters shall prophesy" (Joel 2:28), he was likely talking about preaching God's Word. However, the gift of prophecy is supernatural and can occur in the middle of preaching or at critical moments in the life of an individual or of the church. Let's examine a couple of moments when prophecies are given in the Bible. These two examples are prophecy as foretelling the future.

> During this time some prophets came down from Jerusalem to Antioch. One of them, named Agabus, stood up and through the Spirit, predicted that a

severe famine would spread over the entire Roman world. (This happened during the reign of Claudius.)
—ACTS 11:27–28

The church took this prophecy very seriously and received an offering because of the foretold famine. They wisely listened to the prophets, and God used this word to meet their needs.

Another prophecy is recorded when Paul was on his way to Jerusalem after traveling and spreading the gospel during his final missionary journey. He was approached by Agabus from Judea with a prophecy. "Coming over to us, he took Paul's belt, tied his own hands and feet with it and said, 'The Holy Spirit says, "In this way the Jewish leaders in Jerusalem will bind the owner of this belt and will hand him over to the Gentiles"'" (Acts 21:11).

This prophecy from Agabus was very significant and indeed came true. As an illustration, Agabus took Paul's belt, tied himself, and prophesied that in the same way he was tied, the Jewish leaders would take Paul. In Jerusalem, Paul would be arrested and ultimately arrive in Rome after going through a shipwreck and two years' incarceration in Caesarea.

It is important to note that those standing by in this moment in Ephesus told Paul, "You should not go to Jerusalem. God is telling you not to go." However, Paul said, "No, that's not what God is doing." He understood that God was sending him, and he would go bound in the Spirit to Jerusalem.

In other words, he knew what God was saying to him. He understood that God was giving him a forewarning of what would happen, but he knew in his heart that he was still to go to Jerusalem. He had to discern the word for himself.

Never guiding your life by one prophecy alone is imperative. A prophecy is a word confirming what God is already speaking or preparing you for or what He is about to do, but we should never make decisions on just one prophetic declaration. Paul exhorts us to let every word be established by two or three witnesses (2 Corinthians 13:1).

We do well to remember that prophecy is subject to the person giving it. At our best, people are prejudiced and skewed by the flesh. People who are used in the operation of the gifts of the Spirit are human and can miss it. One of the keys to being used in the gift of prophecy is being willing to admit when you have erred. Now, if you continue to speak in error consistently without repentance, you are a false prophet. We are human. God will use us, but we must stay in touch with our humanity. We are only vessels carrying the true treasure of God's gifts through the Holy Spirit.

Tongues refers to speaking an unknown language.

The gift of tongues is to be interpreted. On the Day of Pentecost in Acts 2 the early church spoke in tongues that were understood by those from around the world who were attending the feast. They spoke known tongues. This would be a display of *xenolalia,* which is a Greek word that refers to speaking in an actual foreign language that others who speak that language can understand. This is an unusual display of the Holy Spirit and is rarely the case when someone is heard speaking in tongues. Most usually, people speak in their personal prayer language, which I call "devotional tongues." Paul writes: "For anyone who speaks in a tongue does not speak to people but to God. Indeed, no one understands them; they utter mysteries by the Spirit" (1 Corinthians 14:2). The Greek word for this is *glossolalia,* referring to speaking in a language unknown to anyone and understood only by God. Devotional tongues primarily edify the believer personally. When praying in tongues, the Holy Spirit is speaking through the believer to God, and no one understands him. The gift of tongues, however, is a special manifestation of glossolalia where the Holy Spirit is speaking through the believer to the church or to an individual. This manifestation is to be interpreted so that the church will have understanding. The difference between devotional tongues and the gift of tongues is whether it is through the believer to God, not to be understood, or from God through the believer to the church to be interpreted.

The supernatural gift of tongues is the Holy Spirit speaking through a person to the body of Christ or another individual. There is also the possibility that God could use this gift to deliver a message to you. Most often in my journey I have seen God use someone to give a message in tongues to a body of believers. When this happens, it differs from everyone praying or worshipping in tongues. This is not simply someone having ecstatic speech, being blessed, and connecting with heaven. Instead, it is the sense that God is in the room speaking, and we need to listen to what He's saying. When this happens, you pray to interpret. This gift is powerful! I've experienced this many times over the years. I have even seen this gift work at times when I am preaching, and it powerfully confirms the message, giving direction and understanding.

Interpretation of tongues is understanding and communicating the meaning of a message in tongues.

Dennis Bennett was an Episcopal priest who received the baptism of the Holy Spirit in the 1960s. He and his wife tell this story in their book *The Holy Spirit and You*.[1] They also explain that every one of the gifts of the Spirit listed in 1 Corinthians 12 was witnessed in the Old Testament and the New Testament, except for two: tongues and interpretation of tongues. God reserved these gifts for the New Testament, first-century church.

Tongues and the interpretation of tongues when manifesting together could be seen as equal to prophecy. One example of this might be: "While they were worshiping the Lord and fasting, the Holy Spirit said, 'Set apart for me Barnabas and Saul for the work to which I have called them'" (Acts 13:2). The Holy Spirit used the proclamation gifts to give the early church direction, and He will use the gifts to do the same for us.

The gifts of the Spirit demonstrate Jesus' ability to minister to a world in need. They also empower our leadership in a supernatural way that only God can. In the next chapter I share a few examples of my experience with the gifts of the Spirit in my leadership journey.

CHAPTER 5

EMPOWERED BY SUPERNATURAL GIFTS

PERSONAL EXPERIENCES

During my leadership journey I have witnessed every supernatural gift of the Spirit mentioned by Paul in 1 Corinthians 12 operate in my life or leadership situations. I want to take you from theory to practical reality by sharing a few of my experiences (one for each gift) with you. These are just a few of the things I have experienced the Holy Spirit doing in my many years of Spirit-empowered leadership. I realize that these occasions are quite subjective and center on my personal experience. However, because I have experienced these supernatural moments over the years, they remain fresh to me and have shown me some ways the Holy Spirit empowers us for leadership with miraculous gifts. (I am withholding comments on the gifts of healing until chapter 12.) My prayer is that this chapter will make you hungry for a greater impact of the Holy Spirit in your life and open you to experiencing the gifts at work in your leadership.

MESSAGE OR WORD OF WISDOM

When I became president of Oral Roberts University in 2013, I gathered a task force to focus on the globalization of ORU. We met several times to discuss how we could utilize technology at the university to impact our world. As a result of one of those discussions, we decided to initiate a project, such as a new space or building, that would serve as an epicenter for our technological advancements. We initiated the process for designing plans, cost analysis, and other components. One day I was walking through a space called the Baby Mabee. It sat next to the Mabee Center, our basketball arena, and had previously been used as a studio for Oral Roberts' live television program. This unique building was one of the largest television studios of its kind, but it had not been fully utilized for many years.

As I walked through the facility, the Holy Spirit gave me a message of wisdom. I sensed the Lord say, "Why don't you use this space to connect to the world? It would recapture Oral's desire to reach around the globe from ORU but in a new way for the twenty-first century."

Out of that message of wisdom was born what is now the Global Learning Center. It houses artificial intelligence, information technology, high-tech classrooms, banquet spaces, and the largest television studio in Oklahoma, which we use in various ways. In the process of reinventing this space, God provided the funds for us to complete it debt-free.

God gave me a message of wisdom in a critical moment, allowing us to move in a new way for a new day, all for His glory. A message of wisdom will help you in your leadership in critical moments if you position your heart to listen to the Holy Spirit.

> *If you walk in the Spirit, God can use you at any moment in the gifts of the Spirit, equipping you to heal, teach, counsel, lead, and minister in ways beyond human ability.*

This gift of the Holy Spirit operating in your leadership is important. Let's say you are a nurse full of the Holy Spirit and one day you walk into a patient's room. Suddenly, the Holy Spirit gives you a word of wisdom about your patient, and that word unlocks their healing. If you are a teacher, you might sense exactly how to explain a difficult concept so a student truly understands, or as a counselor, you may receive insight into the heart of someone struggling and know the right words to guide them. If you walk in the Spirit, God can use you at any moment in the gifts of the Spirit, equipping you to heal, teach, counsel, lead, and minister in ways beyond human ability.

MESSAGE OR WORD OF KNOWLEDGE

Years ago I was traveling on a mission trip through Malaysia. After long days of journeying through the country and ministering in different settings, I was preaching at our last meeting in Kuala Lumpur. After two weeks of pouring out daily in the hot, humid Malaysian climate without air conditioning in the buildings, I was exhausted. After preaching that night, I began praying for people, and a young lady named Jenny was at the end of the prayer line. As I prayed for her, a demon began to manifest. I quickly perceived that she was demon possessed. I asked the team to take her to a back room and minister to her there so she would not disrupt the remainder of the service. They continued praying for her while the pastor and I concluded the gathering.

Following the meeting I was scheduled to get in a car and travel to Singapore to catch my flight home. I was ready! I could not wait to sleep in my bed and have one of my wife, Lisa's home-cooked meals. I knew, however, I should first check on our team in the back room with Jenny. So I slipped behind the stage to witness their prayer time. Jenny was a professional and sharp young lady, but when I opened the door, I saw her in the middle of the floor, screaming profusely with her body twisting and contorting. Demons were clearly manifesting themselves. I could not leave our team in this situation. The car to Singapore would have to wait. I knelt beside Jenny, and as I began praying for her and rebuking the devil, the spiritual battle intensified. In retrospect I believe that several demons were cast out of Jenny during those hours of prayer. The victory would seem to come, and then another enemy would manifest, tormenting her and challenging us.

Finally, around three in the morning, we encountered the last stronghold in Jenny's life, and it was fierce! Nothing I did seemed to be able to break the grip of Satan on Jenny. I knew that I would not make my flight out of Singapore. After hours of praying, I was frustrated, weary, and ready to give up. At that moment, we heard a man's deep voice come from Jenny's mouth and say to me, "You're exhausted, and I'm going to win." We know the devil is a liar; he is the father of all lies (John 8:44). Yet at that moment, he told a partial truth. I was indeed exhausted! Instantaneously, the Holy Spirit rose within me, and I responded immediately without premeditation, "You're right. I am exhausted, but God is not. He is going to win this battle, and you're going to leave in Jesus' name." However, the demon remained. The fight continued. I had never encountered anything like it. I would plead the blood of Jesus, and through Jenny, the demon would say to me, "I plead the blood over you." I would rebuke the demonic spirit in Jesus' name, and it would respond to me, "I rebuke you in Jesus' name." I know for the religious people reading this who have never cast out devils or encountered the enemy at this level, this all sounds absurd. It seemed irrational and strange to me that night; nonetheless, it was real. By around four in the morning, I was perplexed and unsure about what to do.

Suddenly, while I was praying quietly, the Holy Spirit gave me a word of knowledge through a vision. He revealed to me that Jenny had been sexually abused as a child. From that abuse she had become bitter and invited these demons into her life to fight against the abuser. Through this bitterness and pain, the devil entered Jenny's life. I declared this revelation to Jenny, who was also exhausted, and the battle was on its way to a glorious ending.

Immediately, a flood of God's love filled the room, washing over us. I can still recall, even sense, that feeling as I rehearse this account almost thirty-five years later. Instantly, Jenny began to cry, and the demon was gone. She surrendered her life to Jesus on the spot and started serving Him. Years later Jenny remained a good member of the local church and was completely free from her bondage. I could not have known what I declared in those early-morning hours, except by the Holy Spirit. The battle was won through a message of knowledge. I missed my flight from Singapore, but thankfully, I was placed on another one. And I was delighted that the Holy Spirit helped me in my weakness while showing Jesus' power of deliverance to everyone who witnessed our prayer with Jenny that morning.

FAITH

I was preaching at an open-air crusade in Managua, Nicaragua. Nicaragua had recently endured a difficult war, and the people were suffering in many ways. Thousands of people gathered to hear God's Word and find hope. While preaching, I noticed a man who was disabled and in a wheelchair. My faith was not particularly strong at that moment. Over the years, I have not been especially gifted in seeing people raised from wheelchairs. This has only happened a few times in my ministry. God was moving powerfully that night, and through the work of the Holy Spirit, I received a supernatural measure of faith I did not have within myself. I said to the man, "Get up in the name of Jesus and come up on this stage." This man, who had not walked in twenty years, arose from his wheelchair and stepped onto the stage. Seeing God miraculously touch this man was thrilling. Hundreds of people flooded the altar, and Jesus' power was on display. After the crusade I thought, "Where did that faith come from?" I did not improvise or fake it. It was supernatural, and God performed the miracle.

HEALING (SEE CHAPTER 12)

MIRACULOUS POWERS

Years ago I was preaching at a large camp meeting. Several thousand people attended each night, and the services were wonderful. I did not always attend the morning services, but one morning I was sitting on stage during the main session with the state bishop. The service was a little slow (an understatement) with many reports and business matters. Most people seemed half asleep. At one point I looked out and saw a man named Brother Durham and his wife sitting about halfway back in the auditorium. Brother Durham was an iconic pastor in his movement, and I had preached for him several times in the mountains of Kentucky. I was looking in his direction when his wife, Sister Durham, who had been struggling with cancer, fell over on the chairs beside her. At first, I thought she might have been bored or tired and fallen asleep. That was not what happened. She must have been wearing a wig because of the side effects from her chemo treatment, for it fell off, and then she became completely still and began turning very pale. In only a few moments it was obvious that Sister Durham had collapsed and died during the meeting. Immediately, the state bishop stopped the business session and asked if a medical professional was in the venue. A nurse rushed to Sister Durham's side, and they called the EMTs in Frankfort, Kentucky, to come to the convention center.

More than twenty minutes—which seemed like a long time—elapsed before the EMTs arrived. During that time, the nurse was unable to find Sister Durham's pulse because she had stopped breathing. No one knew what to do. The crowd was not overly large, so we formed an informal circle around where Sister Durham was lying on the chairs and began to sing and pray. Understandably, Brother Durham was distressed. His wife had collapsed and died while sitting beside him. The state bishop was trying to help the church through these very awkward moments until the EMTs could retrieve Sister Durham and take her to the morgue.

As we continued singing, one of the pastors was being touched by the Holy Spirit. He was praying loudly in the Spirit and started moving toward Sister Durham's lifeless body. We were not sure what was happening, but when he reached Sister Durham's body, he laid his hands on her head and continued praying in the Spirit. While the pastor was speaking in tongues, we heard Sister Durham make a noise. Immediately, she sat up, grabbed her wig, and was alive and well. After no pulse could be found for over fifteen minutes, God raised her up, and she lived many more years!

The Holy Spirit worked through a man in miraculous power, demonstrating to everyone in that camp meeting session what Jesus can do. The miracle-working gift was witnessed before several hundred people. Honestly, the pastor God used that day would not have been my pick, nor was he considered to be a spiritual giant by most in attendance; however, he knew how to allow Jesus' miraculous Holy Spirit's empowerment to flow through him, and everyone was blessed because of it.

PROPHECY

Many prophecies have been given or spoken to me over the years. Some of them have been true, and some have not. One was a word I received years ago in Romania. I was there preaching, and the meeting was wonderful with a strong attendance in a rural area of the country. God was touching many people. A woman approached me supposedly with a word and said, "You are in extreme danger, and you are to leave Romania now."

This woman seemed very spiritual and godly, a prayer warrior in the church. I first thought, "Wow, that sounds serious." I went back to my room and prayed about this "word." I believe the Lord spoke to me and said, "I didn't tell you that you were in danger. That lady told you that you were in danger. I am moving, and unless I tell you to leave, you need to stay." We had hundreds of people touched in that meeting. After the meeting I left Romania. I never was harmed or felt any sense of danger. It was a false prophecy. You must discern every word that is given to you and never guide your life by one prophecy alone. This is crucial!

While I have received inaccurate prophecies over the years, I have also received accurate ones. The first was when I was sixteen years old. I was newly converted and filled with the Holy Spirit. Having recently reestablished our relationship after years of brokenness, my father and I were taking our first ministry trip together. During that trip, we visited a church in Rockford, Illinois. Dad and I walked to the church building one afternoon to pray together with Pastor Keith, one of Dad's friends.

During our three-person prayer meeting, Pastor Keith laid his hands on my head and spoke prophetically that I would take the gospel of Jesus Christ to the nations of the world. This was a bit heavy for a sixteen-year-old who was on his first trip west of the Mississippi River and had never been on an airplane. We would later laugh about this encounter. Although seemingly strange at that moment, this was indeed a word from the Lord. I always respected Pastor Keith for his spiritual obedience, especially now that I have preached on-site in almost one hundred different nations, and our television program is currently seen in more than 150 nations every week. I also serve as president of ORU, which has had students attend from more than 170 nations in the past six years.

While this was a true prophecy, I did not immediately act on it. I didn't go to the airport and say, "Somebody gave me a prophecy that I'm going all over the world preaching the gospel! Where is my ticket?" I trusted God to bring His words to pass in His timing, and He did. Years later, as I lay in bed in the remote mountains of Sumatra, Indonesia, where I was on my first long-distance mission trip, those words to an inexperienced sixteen-year-old resonated in my heart. I was encouraged by the realization that God knew what He was doing with me long before I did!

DISTINGUISHING BETWEEN SPIRITS (DISCERNMENT)

At another time I was in Mexico at our denominational conference with camp ministry directors from Central and South America. More than one hundred leaders attended. On the last night of the conference, I stood after the worship service to minister from God's Word. The Holy Spirit was moving strongly. It was a powerful time. One of my spiritual mothers, Naomi, was with me and serving as my interpreter.

Suddenly, a lady to the right of the stage started jumping across the floor on her knees like a frog while speaking in tongues. It was extremely strange. I have seen many unique things over the years, but this occasion gave me the willies. She was loud and disrupted the meetings. She would spring up like a frog, land on the floor, and speak in tongues the whole time. Honestly, I thought this was a demonically motivated manifestation that was interrupting my attempt to preach. I said to Naomi, "Let's stop that; we need to pray for this woman." Her response was, "Let's wait a minute and see. It may be God." Surprisingly, she was right.

After the lady finished speaking in tongues, she gave an interpretation. The message was a tremendously strong warning to someone struggling spiritually. The message stated that this was their opportunity to reconcile with God. Immediately, a woman rushed forward from about four rows back, weeping and broken. She approached the stage area to share her story with Naomi and me. The weeping lady served as the wife of one of our national overseers. That night, she confessed to recently having an affair. She repented and turned her heart back to the Lord. We witnessed an amazing moment of salvation and rescue.

Yet if I had followed my natural inclination, we would have missed this significant deliverance. Thankfully, Naomi had better discernment than I did that night. The gift of discernment helped us not miss what the Holy Spirit was doing. The lady who came forward was rescued. Her life was restored, and God saved her marriage. Although she and her husband were required to step away from leadership for a while, they eventually returned to leadership, demonstrating Jesus' ability to know the secrets in our lives and to restore us when we turn to Him.

TONGUES AND INTERPRETATION OF TONGUES

Oral Roberts had an unusual understanding of the gift of tongues and their interpretation. He believed that when you pray in tongues, you could and should interpret for yourself. Roberts stated that he built Oral Roberts University because he walked the fields where the university presently stands, praying in the Spirit and interpreting what the Spirit was saying. God told him what to do and how to do it. I have only experienced this unique interpretation gift a few times. One of the most dramatic times I experienced this was when I was going before the search committee to discuss becoming president of ORU. The night before visiting with the committee, I flew into Dallas-Fort Worth and stayed in a hotel at the airport. The following morning, Lisa called me to share that she had experienced a difficult dream regarding the possibility of serving at ORU. The university was still emerging from a horrific time of crisis, and though I had been serving on the board of trustees as vice chair for five years, Lisa was still very concerned about my taking this significant new step.

That morning, I was in my hotel room when Lisa called and shared her dream with me. Since she is my wife, I felt the urgency to pray about this more before meeting with the committee. I knelt and prayed, and as I did, I began speaking in tongues. During this remarkable, Spirit-empowered moment, I interpreted aloud what the Lord was saying to me. This was an uncommon and powerfully impactful experience for me.

I climbed into bed with tears flowing down my face. I told God that I was unsure if I could do this job. At that time, it was necessary to secure a minimum of between ten and twelve million dollars annually to maintain university operations. In my current ministry, I was raising around $300,000 a year. So I said to the Lord, "I've never done this before." The Holy Spirit said to me, "Do not worry about the money. I will take care of it." After this encounter I knew by the time I arrived at the meeting with the search committee that I was to be president of ORU. When I walked in, I did not tell them, but in my heart I understood it was God's will. God has kept His word, and we have raised an average of twenty-four million dollars a year since I have been the university's president. God has taken care of it as He told me He would.

As repeatedly illustrated in my own life, the gifts of the Spirit operate in unique ways to demonstrate to the world that Jesus is alive and still working in our day. The Bible outlines some simple yet important operational principles for the supernatural gifts of the Spirit.

PRINCIPLES OF OPERATION FOR THE SUPERNATURAL GIFTS

1) Gifts should be demonstrated decently and in order.
2) Gifts should operate under proper authority.
3) Gifts work according to our faith.
4) Gifts are for the edification of the body of believers.
5) Gifts are to glorify Jesus.

> *The gifts of the Spirit are a vital part of the believer's life and a critical component of Spirit-empowered leadership.*

WALKING IN THE GIFTS

The gifts of the Spirit are a vital part of the believer's life and a critical component of Spirit-empowered leadership. Whether ministry gifts, grace gifts, or supernatural gifts, they all serve the same purpose—to glorify Jesus and edify His people. As the body of Christ, we all have different gifts, and yet we complement one another with all members making up one body. "Just as a body, though one, has many parts, but all its many parts form one body, so it is with Christ" (1 Corinthians 12:12). We may not operate in all the gifts, and that is OK. God uses us uniquely, and we need each other (1 Corinthians 12:12–27).

Wherever the Holy Spirit works, the gifts of the Spirit are available. If you are full of the Holy Spirit, you are a candidate to be used in the gifts. Remember, the gifts listed in 1 Corinthians 12 are not residential. Even Oral Roberts, known for his great healing ministry, did not possess the gift of healing. Shortly before he passed, he showed me his right hand and said, "Billy, I've laid this hand on over a million people personally. Thousands of them have been healed, and thousands have not—I'll never understand that." Roberts knew he did not possess the gift, but it belonged to the Holy Spirit. When Roberts died, the gift of healing did not die with him. When the apostle Paul died, the spiritual gifts did not cease.

Paul encouraged us, "Follow the way of love and eagerly desire gifts of the Spirit, especially prophecy" (1 Corinthians 14:1). We should desire, seek to understand, and operate in these gifts with humility and love. May we be a people who walk in both the fruit and the gifts of the Spirit, demonstrating the personality and power of Jesus to a world desperately in need of Him.

CHAPTER 6

THE HEART OF A LEADER

At the core of leadership is not just skill—it is the heart of the leader. Ken Blanchard, a respected leadership expert, once said, "The heart of great leadership is a leader's great heart."[1] Leadership is more than a position; it is the internal condition of the leader that ultimately determines their impact. A leader's external effectiveness is directly tied to their internal strength, values, and character. As Spirit-empowered leaders, we are not merely guided by instinct but by the Holy Spirit, who shapes our decisions and our leadership from within.

A recent analysis of top-performing CEOs revealed a compelling insight into executive decision-making. Despite having access to advanced analytics and data-driven tools, many leaders acknowledged that their most impactful decisions were guided not by metrics alone but by intuition. As Laura Huang notes in *Harvard Business Review,* these CEOs treat intuition as a skill, one honed through experience and reflection. Rather than dismissing gut feelings, they integrate them with data to navigate complex challenges, often finding that their instincts led to their most successful outcomes.[2]

For Spirit-empowered leaders, we do not merely listen to our gut instinct or human intuition but follow the Holy Spirit's prompting. Our intuition is to be formed by Him. Therefore, the most effective way to lead is from within, from a well-formed heart that is in tune with God's voice. Leadership requires decision-making, and we need wisdom beyond our natural understanding.

Mark Miller says, "The heart is a muscle, and you strengthen muscles by using them. The more I lead with my heart, the stronger that it gets."[3] If leadership is rooted in the heart, then what kind of heart must a leader have? Let's explore the essential qualities that should shape a Spirit-empowered leader's heart.

1) A HEART OF PURITY AND INTEGRITY

The writer of Proverbs declares, "Above all else, guard your heart, for everything you do flows from it" (Proverbs 4:23). Ultimately, you will do what is in your heart. Essentially, leaders must guard their hearts to lead well.

Dwight D. Eisenhower, former US president and military leader, said, "The supreme quality of leadership is integrity."[4] Inner stability is key to leadership. Ray Kroc, who helped expand McDonald's into a global company, said, "The quality of a leader is reflected in the standards they set for themselves."[5]

You must consider what standards you will set for yourself and the nonnegotiables by which you will live and lead.

Billy Graham was a great example of this principle. His ministry was marked by honesty, transparency, and integrity. Early in his career, Graham and his team established the *Modesto Manifesto* while in a hotel room in Modesto, California, in 1948. The manifesto was a set of guidelines for the ministry to ensure integrity in financial matters, media reporting, and personal conduct. This commitment to integrity safeguarded his ministry from scandal and established him as one of the most trusted Christian leaders of all time.[6]

Modesto Manifesto

"We settle in our hearts and minds the determination that integrity will be the hallmark of both our lives and our ministry."
1948 - Billy Graham, Cliff Barrows, George Beverly Shea & Grady Wilson

Resolutions that will guide us in future evangelistic work. A commitment to do all we can do to uphold the Bible's standard of absolute integrity and purity for evangelists

1. We will avoid financial abuses, downplay offerings & have financial accountability
2. We will avoid any situation that would have even the appearance of compromise or suspicion of sexual immorality
3. We will partner with all who would cooperate in the public proclamation of the Gospel. We will avoid any antichurch or anticlergy attitude, refusing to criticize local churches and pastors
4. We will commit to integrity in our publicity and our reporting by avoiding the exaggeration of successes and attendance numbers

The Youth Committee for the Jacksonville Billy Graham Crusade
November 2-5, 2000

In my ministry I have certain boundaries to safeguard myself and the ministry God has entrusted to me. For example, I will not counsel a female one-on-one behind closed doors, nor do I travel alone with someone from the opposite sex. Setting clear guardrails and standards is vital, even when it seems unnecessary. I have had televisions taken out of my hotel room during crusades. I have had people check my internet activity, and now, with current technology, Lisa can track me at all times. Establishing standards for the sake of purity is important.

Integrity is not just about avoiding wrongdoing; it is also about actively choosing what is right, even when difficult. Leaders must ask themselves, "Am I leading in a way that aligns with my values and God's standards?"

2) A HEART OF COURAGE

Leadership requires courage. Robert Louis Stevenson once said, "Keep your fears to yourself, but share your courage with others."[7] Courageous leaders inspire their teams to move forward. Scripture reveals that God calls leaders to demonstrate courage. When Joshua was entrusted with leading Israel into the Promised Land, God commanded him, "Be strong and courageous. Do not be afraid; do not be discouraged, for the LORD your God will be with you wherever you go" (Joshua 1:9). Leadership requires the ability to step forward in faith, even when it is challenging.

3) A HEART OF PASSION

Passion fuels great leadership. Confucius stated, "Wherever you go, go with all your heart."[8] Leaders who are passionate about their mission naturally inspire others to follow. Passion is contagious, igniting others around you to lead with enthusiasm and commitment.

A Spirit-empowered leader pursues God's calling with zeal. Paul's letter to the Colossian believers encourages us, "Whatever you do, work at it with all your heart, as working for the Lord, not for human masters" (Colossians 3:23). Passionate leadership is done wholeheartedly. You will know a dream is from God when it ignites passion and inspiration. This passion will be the fuel that keeps you going. Cardinal James Gibbons said, "There are no office hours for leaders."[9] Of course, leaders need to stay healthy and balance their work, family, and rest well. Yet the truth is that leadership has no real office hours. You are always a leader. You cannot be both lazy and a good leader.

4) A RESTFUL HEART

While leadership requires passion, it also requires a heart at rest in God. A leader who lacks peace will struggle to bring peace to their team. Paul advised his spiritual son, "The servant of the Lord must not strive; but be gentle unto all men, apt to teach, patient" (2 Timothy 2:24, KJV).

True rest and peace come from trusting God's providence and guidance. The psalmist Asaph reminds us, "No one from the east or the west or from the desert can exalt themselves. It is God who judges: He brings one down, He exalts another" (Psalm 75:6–7). Leaders who trust God's timing and direction avoid the anxiety of striving for position and recognition. Promotion comes from the Lord. Be a person of passion, integrity, and excellence, and trust God to exalt you in due time (1 Peter 5:6). You will not need to manipulate your way into a position. Remember, if man puts you in, man can take you out, but if God puts you in, only God can take you out. This truth will bring great peace to your heart.

This is how I feel about my job as president of ORU. I did not ask for the job. The truth is that I said no to this position a few times. I am serving in this role because God's design was to put me here, and that gives me great peace. Of course, the board can remove me, but I do not concern myself with that. I trust God wherever He places me. I have never been fired from a job, but I have had difficult transitions. I have learned to rest in the fact that God is in control. Having this peace makes you a strong leader.

Courageous leadership is secure leadership. Insecurity cannot lead. If a leader is insecure, others can sense their uncertainty, and their team will not follow. You must come to a deep place of rest in God and do away with the fear of man.

| *Courageous leadership is secure leadership.* |

5) A HUMBLE HEART

Humility is rare in secular leadership. Yet the best leaders are humble. Humility is the opposite of pride, not self-exalting, and the foundation for great leadership. Rick Warren wisely wrote, "Humility is not thinking less of yourself, it is thinking of yourself less."[10] True humility does not involve self-degradation but merely shifts the focus from self to serving others.

Humble leaders admit mistakes. We are human, and we will err from time to time. Owning our failures and remaining humble is vital for good leadership. Seek counsel and prioritize the needs of those you lead.

Lolly Daskal, CEO of her organization Lead from Within, shared in a blog post what a humble leader looks like:

- They lead to serve.
- They have reserves of inner strength.
- They admit their mistakes.
- They seek input from others.
- They know themselves.
- They are genuine.
- They invite trust.
- They treat others with respect.
- They understand their limitations.
- They model the way.[11]

Spirit-empowered leaders must lead with a humble heart.

6) A COMPASSIONATE HEART

Teddy Roosevelt once stated, "People don't care how much you know until they know how much you care."[12] I have found this to be true. Compassionate leaders connect with people on a deep level. Paul instructs us to "rejoice with those who rejoice; mourn with those who mourn" (Romans 12:15).

> *A great leader not only celebrates victories but also stands with others in their struggles.*

A great leader not only celebrates victories but also stands with others in their struggles. The psalmist declares, "Those who sow with tears will reap with songs of joy. Those who go out weeping, carrying seed to sow, will return with songs of joy, carrying sheaves with them" (Psalm 126:5–6). I have learned in my life that when I come to a place of prayer and compassion for the people I am ministering to, I will reap a harvest. If I go into a pulpit with a hardened heart, I will experience barrenness. Our hearts must be sensitized to those around us and care for them the way God does. This principle is vital in ministry, business, and life. Whether comforting a grieving employee, encouraging a struggling student, or investing in a broken community, leaders who show genuine compassion leave a lasting impact.

One of the most powerful illustrations of this is found in Victor Hugo's novel *Les Misérables*. I have seen the musical adaptation on Broadway, in Tulsa, and on television several times. It is one of my all-time favorites and always touches me deeply. The story takes place in nineteenth-century France and follows Jean Valjean, a former convict who is given a second chance at life through the kindness of a priest. Valjean is transformed into an honorable man, becomes the mayor of a small town, and is a business owner. He hires a woman named Fantine, who has a daughter, Cosette. When the workers at the factory find out that Fantine had her child out of wedlock, they reject her and cause turmoil. Valjean ultimately releases her from the company. Fantine finds herself on the streets, doing whatever it takes to take care of her daughter. First, she sells her hair, then her teeth, and finally her body. Her tragic story, encapsulated in the song "I Dreamed a Dream," illustrates the harsh realities that many people in our world face when life does not go as expected and they lose hope.

Fantine had a dream. She dreamed of a life with the father of her child. When he left her, she found herself doing what she never dreamed she would do. Many people in the world are hurting in this same way. Most people in prostitution, prisons, and homelessness on the street never intended to be there. Something in life happened to them, and their dreams were stolen. Until you learn to hurt and empathize with those who are hurting, you will be unable to reach them for Christ. Compassion will lead you to show the broken that they can find a new dream in Jesus. When leaders allow their hearts to be moved by the pain of others, they become instruments of healing and transformation. When was the last time you wept over hurting people? When was the last time you were moved with compassion toward those you lead?

The heart of a leader determines the effectiveness of their leadership. A Spirit-empowered leader possesses a heart of integrity, courage, passion, rest, humility, and compassion.

CHAPTER 7

LESSONS FROM A YOUNG LEADER

As a young leader, I was significantly blessed by the life and ministry of Timothy. I studied and read about his journey, learning a great deal about leadership. Timothy was apostle Paul's spiritual son in the faith, a travel partner, a missionary, a pastor, and a leader in the early church. His life and ministry provide invaluable lessons for young leaders today.

A few years ago a Universum study surveyed different generations—Gen X, Gen Y (millennials), and Gen Z—about their leadership aspirations. The research found that Gen Z values leadership but struggles with the stress that comes with responsibility. Interestingly, Gen Z ranked "high levels of responsibility" as a desirable leadership trait while simultaneously citing "high levels of stress" as a major deterrent to leadership roles.[1]

This contrast highlights a key challenge for today's young leaders. Leadership is not just about influence. As you are given more responsibility, you will experience more pressure, stress, and sacrifice. Timothy's life demonstrated this. He experienced numerous stressful situations, yet he modeled how young leaders embrace responsibility while navigating leadership challenges with resilience and empowerment through the Holy Spirit. I will share several key leadership lessons identified from an analysis of Timothy's life.

LESSON 1: UNDERSTAND THE FAMILY EFFECT

Family makes a difference in leadership. Luke relates when Paul first encountered young Timothy: "Paul came to Derbe and then to Lystra, where a disciple named Timothy lived, whose mother was Jewish and a believer but whose father was a Greek" (Acts 16:1). Luke specifically notes that Timothy was born into a mixed household because it shaped his identity. His mother, Eunice, and grandmother, Lois, were devout believers from a Jewish background, and their faith played an important role in Timothy's spiritual formation. Paul encouraged Timothy by saying, "I am reminded of your sincere faith, which first lived in your grandmother Lois and in your mother Eunice and, I am persuaded, now lives in you also" (2 Timothy 1:5). Although we are not given many details about Timothy's father, he was a Gentile and most likely a polytheistic Greek.

Many scholars believe Timothy's father passed away when he was young or was absent much of Timothy's life, which opened Timothy to receiving Paul as a spiritual father and mentor. Timothy's family reality highlights an essential leadership principle: Your family, whether strong in faith or broken in sin, affects your leadership. Every family story can dramatically impact you; consequently, understanding how your family shapes you as a leader can make you more effective.

Timothy's background uniquely prepared him for his ministry to the Gentiles. His Jewish heritage gave him credibility among Jewish believers, while his Greek lineage positioned him to connect with non-Jews. As leaders, our family background always informs our journey.

My grandfather, a great Pentecostal preacher and man of God, left a strong legacy of faith. I was called into ministry at his funeral when I was eleven. During the service I was standing by his casket when a relative said, "Nobody will ever preach like M. E. Wilson." The Holy Spirit touched me, and tears filled my eyes. I responded, "Oh yes, they will." In that moment, I knew deep in my heart that someday I would preach the gospel. I can still feel the power of that calling today!

Understanding your family legacy and background is important. Some believers do not come from a family of faith, but they are given the chance to form a new generational lineage. However, understanding your background is crucial to shaping your leadership journey.

LESSON 2: ESTEEM THE POWER OF YOUR REPUTATION

Luke continued by telling us of Timothy's impact on others: "The believers at Lystra and Iconium spoke well of him" (Acts 16:2). Your reputation is one of the most valuable assets you possess. The wise writer of Proverbs declares, "A good name is more desirable than great riches; to be esteemed is better than silver or gold" (Proverbs 22:1). The question is, What do people say about you? While you should not idolize other people's opinions of you, you also cannot completely negate what others say. To be a valued, Spirit-empowered leader, you must have a good reputation.

> *Your character and reputation will either enhance or hinder your leadership opportunities.*

Paul also exhorted Timothy, "Don't let anyone look down on you because you are young, but set an example for the believers in speech, in conduct, in love, in faith, and in purity" (1 Timothy 4:12). As a young leader, how you are known by friends, classmates, professors, mentors, and others in your sphere of influence can open or close doors. Your character and reputation will either enhance or hinder your leadership opportunities. How do you talk? Do you cuss and gossip? How is your conduct? Are you lazy or hardworking? How do you treat others? Do you go out of your way to show love, or are you selfish and self-serving? Do you have faith? Can you endure difficult times and persist in maintaining a strong trust in God? Are you pure? Do you live a godly lifestyle? One of the reasons Paul invited Timothy on his missionary journeys was that the young man's reputation preceded him. Others spoke well of Timothy because of his conduct, love, faith, and purity.

LESSON 3: EXPAND YOUR PAIN AND SACRIFICE THRESHOLD

Timothy had to expand his capacity for pain and sacrifice in order to lead. Remember, Timothy was from Lystra. This was the same city where Paul was stoned and left for dead (Acts 14:19). Timothy saw firsthand what it might mean to serve Jesus and chose to follow anyway.

In the Acts narrative about Timothy, Luke presents one of the more astonishing verses in Scripture: "Paul wanted to take him [Timothy] along on the journey, so he circumcised him because of the Jews who lived in that area, for they all knew that his father was a Greek" (Acts 16:3).

This is surprising because the Jerusalem Council had declared that Gentiles did not need circumcision to follow Christ (cf. Acts 15). Yet Paul required Timothy to undergo this painful procedure as a young adult. Why? Because Timothy's mixed heritage meant he would minister among both Jews and Gentiles. Paul understood that removing this potential offense would enable Timothy to be more effective with the Jewish population. I suspect that if we told young adult Christian males the prerequisite for entry into ministry was a crude operation on their private parts without anesthesia, performed by a preacher rather than a surgeon, the number of ministerial applicants would fall to an all-time low. However, Timothy submitted and was willing to endure the pain required to lead. He would be circumcised so he could travel with Paul and tell gentile converts that they did not have to be circumcised.

Leadership requires self-sacrifice and at times pain. The cost of leadership can be very personal. Sometimes others can, but you cannot. Paul later told Timothy, "Join with me in suffering, like a good soldier of Christ Jesus" (2 Timothy 2:3). A low pain threshold can lead to a low leadership potential. To lead effectively, you must be willing to endure hardship. To be a leader, you must be willing to suffer the pain necessary to lead. If you cannot endure pain, you cannot be a leader.

LESSON 4: ALWAYS REMAIN A STUDENT

Paul instructs Timothy, "Study to shew thyself approved unto God, a workman that needeth not to be ashamed, rightly dividing the word of truth" (2 Timothy 2:15, KJV). He exhorts Timothy to learn from God and him as a seasoned apostle.

This spiritual father wrote to his son in the faith: "Until I come, devote yourself to the public reading of Scripture, to preaching and to teaching. Do not neglect your gift, which was given you through prophecy when the body of elders laid their hands on you" (1 Timothy 4:13–14).

Great leaders are lifelong learners. Always be a student, seeking to grow in knowledge, understanding, and wisdom. A learning posture will set you apart and keep you effective in your calling.

> *Great leaders are lifelong learners.*

LESSON 5: RELEASE THE POWER OF HONOR

Paul taught Timothy the importance of honor in leadership: "Do not rebuke an older man harshly, but exhort him as if he were your father. Treat younger men as brothers, older women as mothers, and younger women as sisters, with absolute purity" (1 Timothy 5:1–2). He also reminded him, "The elders who direct the affairs of the church well are worthy of double honor" (1 Timothy 5:17).

I was appointed as the Church of God of Prophecy International Youth Ministries director at the ripe old age of twenty-four. At that time, everyone on the denomination's executive leadership team was over forty, most were over sixty, except me; I believe that I was the youngest denominational executive in the church's history. I was excited to serve Jesus, but to be honest, I did not know much about what I was doing. My first weeks on the job were quite intimidating. I remember reading 1 and 2 Timothy almost every week because I needed to know how to serve among older believers, many of whom were my spiritual heroes. These epistles from Paul to Timothy guided me, and I began inviting those around me to be my spiritual parents by asking questions about life and ministry. They were excited that I came to them for counsel. I honored them every chance I could, and I had amazing favor among them because I chose to honor them. This was Timothy's approach. He was assigned by Paul to pastor a very mature church in Ephesus. Paul exhorted him to treat these older saints as his spiritual family and give honor to everyone.

Another Scripture that further highlights honor is a difficult passage to exegete:

> All who are under the yoke of slavery should consider their masters worthy of full respect, so that God's name and our teaching may not be slandered. Those who have believing masters should not show them disrespect just because they are fellow believers. Instead, they should serve them even better because their masters are dear to them as fellow believers and are devoted to the welfare of their slaves. These are the things you are to teach and insist on.
> —1 Timothy 6:1–2

Slavery is wrong, but it existed during Timothy's time. Paul even taught slaves to handle their difficult situation with honor.

Writing to the persecuted church and Jewish diaspora in Asia Minor, Peter exhorted them to "show proper respect to everyone, love the family of believers, fear God, honor the emperor" (1 Peter 2:17). These early Christians were facing significant adversity and persecution from Rome. Yet Peter instructed them to honor the emperor. Recognizing that these believers living under difficult rulers were exhorted to honor authority, we should also honor our leaders, even when it is difficult.

You may be in a job where the boss or people in authority over you are dishonorable or unworthy of honor. Yet God's Word tells us to honor anyway. Remember, honor is not about the person but the position they hold. Honor does not mean aiding someone's sin, but you can find ways to honor even dishonorable people, and God will bless you.

David learned this lesson while under the leadership of King Saul, who wanted to kill him before David could ascend to the throne for which Samuel had already anointed the young leader. At one point in the narrative, David encountered Saul in a cave and cut off a portion of the king's robe, shaming the king, who was relieving himself. David was conscience-stricken and said to his men (who felt God had given Saul into David's hand): "The LORD forbid that I should do such a thing to my master, the LORD's anointed, or lay my hand on him; for he is the anointed of the LORD" (1 Samuel 24:6). After sharply rebuking his men, David did not allow them to attack King Saul, who went on his way unharmed.

When you release honor, God's favor will rest upon you. God loves honor.

My first ministry assignment after college was given to me by Fred Fisher Sr., who was serving as the denominational state overseer in Kentucky. Bishop Fisher asked me to serve as state evangelist and later as the state youth director. He was extremely influential in my early years of ministry. I traveled throughout the state of Kentucky and spent numerous hours with the Fishers, both in meetings and at their home in the middle of the state, because it was a good stopping point for me during my travels. The Fishers were wonderful hosts, and we had a great time together. All the while, they were mentoring me and pouring into my life. Many years later Bishop Fisher was a member of the church I pastored in Cleveland, Tennessee, and later became general overseer for our denomination. While I have had numerous mentors and spiritual advisers throughout the years, Brother Fisher was among the first and remained very special and highly respected by both Lisa and me.

A few years ago the Church of God of Prophecy General Assembly was being held in Oklahoma City. Although we had departed from the denomination many years prior, Lisa and I decided to visit. We enjoyed seeing friends and spiritual family again. While we were preparing to travel from Tulsa to Oklahoma City for our one-night visit, I sensed the Holy Spirit nudging me to take a moment and write a check. The check was written for a significant amount to Fred Fisher Sr.

I was attempting to follow God's leading and perhaps find a way to honor someone who had blessed my life. As I left my house in Tulsa, I whispered a prayer that if I saw Brother Fisher, I would deliver my offering and know that I had heard from God. Conversely, if I did not see him, I would merely dismiss the notion as a wrong impression and cancel the check. I put the check in my pocket, and we headed to Oklahoma City.

When Lisa and I arrived at the convention center downtown, we found parking and made our way toward the evening service. This was awkward for us, as it was our first time visiting a general assembly after leaving the denomination. General assemblies were a big part of our life for many years, and I preached in thirteen consecutive assemblies while serving at the denominational offices. We were on familiar ground but experiencing unfamiliar emotions. As we made our way to the convention center, we stepped into the large pre-ballroom area, crowded with people arriving for the service. The first familiar faces we saw were Fred and Betty Fisher. Brother Fisher had retired by this time, and we were delighted to reconnect for a few moments. Of course, I was also thrilled that I had heard from God before leaving home and was honored to place the offering in Brother Fisher's hand while sharing my gratitude for his love for me, especially as a young preacher starting my ministry. It was a special, unique moment that was blessed by God's presence. This was also the last time I would ever see Brother Fisher alive. I was so grateful to have heard God's voice and obeyed. More importantly, I was grateful that

I could tangibly honor one of my elders and spiritual fathers. God loves honor.

LESSON 6: DEMONSTRATE LOYALTY

In *The Fellowship of the Ring,* J. R. R. Tolkien wrote: "Faithless is he that says farewell when the road darkens."[2] Unlike John Mark, who abandoned Paul and Barnabas when the journey became too difficult, Timothy exemplified loyalty. "Barnabas wanted to take John, also called Mark, with them, but Paul did not think it wise to take him, because he had deserted them in Pamphylia and had not continued with them in the work" (Acts 15:37–38). The biblical account reveals that the division between Barnabas and Paul regarding this disagreement was so strong that they parted ways. Following this conflict, Paul found himself in Derbe and Lystra, looking for a new young man to mentor and travel with him. He needed someone who would not run when the pressure was on—someone who would remain faithful, even in difficult circumstances.

A few years after I began following Jesus, I attended a youth conference where a lady named Beatrice preached. I would not describe her as the greatest preacher, but her message captured my heart, and I still remember it fifty years later. She preached from this story about John Mark and Timothy, and asked the question, "Are you a John Mark? Will you run when the pressure's on and quit when it gets tough? Or are you a Timothy? Will you be faithful even when it's difficult?" That day, I said in my heart, "I want to be like Timothy. I want to be faithful even when the journey is tough."

At the end of his life, Paul wrote from prison to Timothy and said:

> Do your best to come to me quickly, for Demas, because he loved this world, has deserted me and has gone to Thessalonica. Crescens has gone to Galatia, and Titus to Dalmatia. Only Luke is with me. Get Mark and bring him with you, because he is helpful to me in my ministry. I sent Tychicus to Ephesus. When you come, bring the cloak that I left with Carpus at Troas, and my scrolls, especially the parchments.
> —2 TIMOTHY 4:9–14

Timothy was faithful to Paul throughout his ministry. Although John Mark had not been faithful earlier, Paul forgave him and invited him to come with Timothy. He wanted to see his earliest spiritual son.

Toward the end of his ministry, Paul needed Timothy more than Timothy needed him. Paul chose the right person that day in Derbe and Lystra to be his spiritual son. I pray the same is true for my spiritual fathers throughout the years.

Loyalty is a rare but essential leadership quality. Will you be loyal to those in leadership over you in the Lord? Will you endure difficult times—the shipwrecks, imprisonments, and dark times? Walter Lippmann stated, "The final test of a leader is that he leaves behind him in other men the conviction and will to carry on."[3] A true leader remains steadfast, even when the journey is difficult.

LESSON 7: ACCESS COURAGE

Timothy struggled with timidity, but Paul called him to embrace courage: "For this reason I remind you to fan into flame the gift of God, which is in you through the laying on of my hands. For the Spirit God gave us does not make us timid, but gives us power, love, and self-discipline" (2 Timothy 1:6–7).

Paul left Timothy with a final charge: "But you, man of God, flee from all this and pursue righteousness, godliness, faith, love, endurance and gentleness. Fight the good fight of the faith. Take hold of the eternal life to which you were called when you made your good confession in the presence of many witnesses" (1 Timothy 6:11–12). Leadership requires boldness. The road will not always be easy, but leaders must rise to the challenge with faith and courage.

CONCLUSION

Timothy's journey teaches us these invaluable leadership lessons: recognize the impact of your family, guard your reputation, endure pain and sacrifice, remain a lifelong student, show honor, demonstrate loyalty, and access courage.

CHAPTER 8

CRITICAL ASSETS EVERY LEADER NEEDS

Every leader carries a toolbox. Some tools are obvious ones—communication, delegation, and time management. Others are deeper, forged in the fire of prayer, adversity, vision, and obedience. Throughout my years of leading, I have learned that successful leadership is not merely about skills or charisma. It is about the assets within you and around you that shape how you lead and what legacy you leave.

In this section I will walk you through what I believe are six critical assets every Spirit-empowered leader must cultivate.

1) A COMPELLING VISION

If you want to lead, you must know where you are going and why it matters. God's Word tells us, "Where there is no vision, the people perish" (Proverbs 29:18, KJV). The first critical asset of a great leader is a compelling vision. Vision is not simply a set of objectives. Vision is what burns in your spirit, compels you forward, and inspires others to run with you. Speaking to the prophet Habakkuk, God said, "Write the vision, and make it plain upon tables, that he may run that readeth it" (Habakkuk 2:2, KJV). Your vision must be clear, writable, shareable, and motivating for you before it moves others.

Ask yourself several questions:

1) *What am I trying to accomplish?* You should have a clear sense of what your goal is.
2) *Does it inspire me?* Others will join you only if you are enthusiastic about your vision.
3) *Can I put my vision into words?* As God impresses you, write down what you believe He is saying, and let His inspiration be your guide.
4) *How are people responding?* If your vision is compelling, others will come alongside and want to be involved.
5) *What will change or happen, or what good will be achieved if the vision is realized?* If you start with the end in mind, you have a greater possibility of reaching your goal.

A compelling vision begins with clarity of calling and conviction before it can become a reality. Mark Twain said, "You can't depend on your eyes when your imagination is out of focus."[1] Vision clears the fog and gives you spiritual sight.

2) A PRACTICAL PLAN

Vision without execution will lead you nowhere. A leader must synergize big dreams with a practical plan.

In his usual wit Yogi Berra once said, "If you don't know where you're going, you'll end up someplace else."[2] Actually, that is painfully true. Without a defined plan, vision drifts into idealism, but a plan turns a dream into an achievable mission.

At ORU we have learned not only to dream big but also to adopt practical short-term and long-term plans for the university's future. During my 2018 summer prayer time God began depositing in me a vision of what ORU could look like by 2030. From that season of prayer and listening, God birthed a visionary thrust called *Impact 2030*. As I began to communicate my heart vision, our teams at ORU started working toward formulating practical plans to be embodied in our *5 Year Adaptive Plan*. We use the term *adaptive* because our strategies are adjusted each year based on prayer, evaluation, the current environment, and the previous year's performance. Our current adaptive plan has eight Goals, forty Objectives, and more than 200 Key Performance Indicators (KPIs). Our eight goals are aimed at 2030 and will remain solid throughout the decade.

They include:

1) Developing Whole Leaders for the Whole World
2) Achieving Exceptional Teaching, Innovation, and Academic Excellence
3) Educating Learners from Every Nation
4) Demonstrating a Vibrant Spirit-Empowered Ethos that Impacts the World
5) Growing a Strong and Expanded Tulsa Campus
6) Using New Technologies in Creative and Transformative Ways
7) Thriving with Financial Vitality
8) Serving Globally as the Premier University for Spirit-Empowered Leadership Development

The objectives are structured as five-year goals that align with and move us toward eight larger targets. Our KPIs change yearly as we work toward meeting each performance measurement. We have a team called the University Planning Council, composed of an equal number of faculty, administration, and trustees, that meets twice a year to review the plan and work on our KPIs for the following year. After completing their work, the board of trustees reviews, amends, and adopts the plan each year for the administration to implement. We are engaged in a robust and rigorous journey! Our *5 Year Adaptive Plan* is not just a document but a road map that drives our institution's growth, excellence, reputation, and global reach. We are well on our way to accomplishing our *Impact 2030* vision because we have a plan that the university works on together to achieve.

To be a successful leader, you need a plan. Whether you are starting a business, running a medical practice, planting a local church, or leading a small group ministry, you need a practical, doable, measurable plan. Your plan will help you and your team accomplish the vision God has given you. As the adage says, "Failing to plan is planning to fail."

> *To be a successful leader, you need a plan.*

Theodore Roosevelt once said, "Keep your eyes on the stars and your feet on the ground."[3] While your vision helps you dream of what is possible, your plan is your grounding and what keeps you from drifting when things get chaotic. Brian Tracy wrote, "A clear vision, backed by definite plans, gives you a tremendous feeling of confidence and personal power."[4]

The key elements of a practical plan include:

- Broad buy-in
- Practical steps
- Consistent reporting
- Regular evaluation

- Periodic adjustments
- Celebration moments
- Continually repeated steps

A practical plan is one of your keys to success.

3) A COMMITTED TEAM

Leadership always requires a team. It is that simple. If no one is following you, you are not leading.

Peter Drucker said, "Unless commitment is made, there are only promises and hopes; but no plans."[5] Great teams are not only talented; they are committed to their mission and one another. Whether the leaders are Moses with Aaron, Miriam, and the seventy elders; David with his thirty mighty men and the loyal warriors who stood by him in caves and battlefields; Jesus with His twelve disciples—each handpicked, diverse, and imperfect yet empowered to carry the gospel; or Paul with a rotating team of faithful companions such as the physician Luke, the young protégé Timothy, and the encourager Barnabas, leadership is always executed through a team.

Each biblical leader accomplished far more through partnership than they ever could alone. Moses needed Aaron and Hur's strength to hold up his hands so that Joshua could win the victory in the valley (Exodus 17:12). He needed Miriam's prophetic song to bring corporate celebration and the elders' wisdom to help govern the people. David did not defeat armies by himself; he had warriors who risked their lives on his behalf (2 Samuel 23:13–17). Jesus invested in disciples who would one day turn the world upside down. Paul traveled with companions who supported, recorded, preached, strengthened the churches, and stood with him in adversity.

Great leaders do not just attract talent; they empower it. They build teams marked by mutual trust, shared vision, and spiritual unity. As a leader, you must ask, "Who is committed to being on my team?"

We have an incredible ORU team. When the Higher Learning Commission, our highest educational accreditor, visited recently, they were amazed not only by the sophistication of our planning process but by the consistency and longevity of our team. Many have served alongside me for more than a decade. That kind of unity and loyalty is not accidental but nurtured.

Andrew Carnegie said it well: "Teamwork is the ability to work together toward a common vision. The ability to direct individual accomplishments toward organizational objectives. It is the fuel that allows common people to attain uncommon results."[6]

Teamwork makes the dream work! Ken Blanchard said, "None of us is as smart as all of us,"[7] and President Ronald Reagan said, "The greatest leader is not necessarily the one who does the greatest things. He is the one who gets the people to do the greatest things."[8]

As you build a team, ask yourself:

- What is the unity level of my team?
- Are people placed in their areas of giftedness?

- Who are the strongest leaders on the team, and how do I work with them?
- Where are the weak spots and recurring conflicts? How do I resolve this?
- What is our collective energy level?
- What is the ethos or culture of our team?

After hearing from God, the most important decision you make as a leader is choosing your team. Jesus prayed all night before selecting the apostles (Luke 6:12–16). Choosing the people who will help achieve your vision is crucial and requires direction from the Holy Spirit, even if you must pray all night. Mark records, "And He appointed twelve [disciples], so that they would be with Him [for instruction] and so that He could send them out to preach [the gospel as apostles—that is, as His special messengers, personally chosen representatives] (Mark 3:14, AMP). The disciples spent approximately two years building relationships and learning from Jesus before He sent them out to minister because He understood the importance of relationally connecting, training, and developing a healthy ethos among His team.

4) A RESOURCE STRATEGY

A big vision requires big provision. You cannot build God-sized dreams with man-sized wallets. When pursuing an initiative, the bottom line usually becomes the top line. An effective leadership strategy relies on efficiently acquiring and stewarding resources.

Paul, Joshua, Nehemiah, David, and other leaders in the Bible all developed a strong resource strategy.

When David prepared the resources for Solomon's temple, he gave from his wealth and inspired the leaders of Israel to contribute as well (1 Chronicles 29:1–9). The result was an outpouring of generosity among the people, bringing great joy. "The people rejoiced at the willing response of their leaders, for they had given freely and wholeheartedly to the Lord" (1 Chronicles 29:9).

Often the most significant difference between achieving a vision and failing to achieve your vision depends on obtaining and stewarding resources effectively. Here are a few resource strategies I have adopted so that the visions God has given me could become reality:

- **Have multiple streams of income.** At ORU we do not rely on student tuition income alone. We have real estate income, donations, a television network, and other creative resource streams. Multiple channels of resources provide greater stability so that if one stream of income diminishes, you still have sources to utilize for sustainability and growth.
- **Understand that vision brings provision.** If you can articulate and live a compelling vision, people will want to give to it.
- **Stewardship is paramount.** Integrity and impact attract generosity and God's continued blessings. Always maintain integrity with those who donate or invest in your work. Tell

the truth, do what you say you are going to do, and report the results of their trust.
- **Personal investment matters.** What are you contributing financially to the effort? Do not expect others to give if you have not invested yourself.
- **Donors care principally about two things: impact and integrity.**

The writer of Proverbs reminds us, "The world of the generous gets larger and larger; the world of the stingy gets smaller and smaller" (Proverbs 11:24, MSG). This scriptural principle changed my life. I discovered that as I moved into radical generosity, God expanded my world and work. If God can trust you with the resources He places in your hands, He will entrust you with more.

5) A STRONG RESOLVE

Leadership is not for the faint of heart. When the going gets tough, you will be tempted to quit. Leaders must face challenges without fear and remain persistent. Robert Jarvik said, "Leaders are visionaries with a poorly developed sense of fear and no concept of the odds against them."[9] In other words, you must believe beyond reason. Courage is especially vital for leadership in the twenty-first century. We are living in turbulent times, and Jesus described days filled with great drama and trauma before His return (Matthew 24). Through it all leaders must be people of stability and bravery. Alexander the Great is quoted as saying, "I am not afraid of an army of lions led by a sheep; I am afraid of an army of sheep led by a lion."[10]

Leaders must face challenges without fear and remain persistent.

Leaders are change agents, and many people resist change. Essentially, if you lead well, some people will not like you. That is why a strong resolve matters. If you need everyone to approve of you, you will not endure, or if you are easily discouraged, you will never finish your race. Your ability to withstand criticism and pain will be critical to leadership success.

Enduring pain is essential in leadership and prepares individuals for greater exploits. While playing basketball in high school, I learned the importance of playing with pain. My grandmother, whom I lovingly called Mammy, helped raise me and repeatedly drilled this statement into me: "Billy, don't ever quit." I was not the strongest basketball player on the court; my ankles were weak, my frame was thin, and I was regularly bruised under the basket. Yet even when my ankles were swollen and taped or the bruises from the last game were not yet healed, I continued to play. I learned to play with pain. This lesson has served me well over the years.

You will have to do the same as a leader. You will experience betrayal, disappointment, delays, and dead ends. You will sometimes wonder if you are doing the right thing. If you keep going, keep playing, and keep leading, you will discover that victory is on the other side of the suffering.

You also must transfer that resolve to your team. When Paul was shipwrecked, he did not panic. He received a word from

God and said, "Not one of you will be lost" (Acts 27:22). He steadied the ship with spiritual authority. As a leader, you will have to do the same. Amid the storm you must speak life and peace to those you lead. Your determination, courage, and resilience will empower them to continue serving even when it hurts.

6) A POWERFUL PARTNER

The most important asset that any leader could possess is the powerful partnership of the Holy Spirit. You can have the best vision, clearest plan, most gifted team, largest budget, and fiercest resolve, but without the Holy Spirit your leadership will not reach its full potential.

The Holy Spirit is the comforter, teacher, and wisdom of God in every moment. He opens doors no man can shut and knows where you should and should not go. If you partner with Him, you will ultimately win, one way or another. He may take you through difficult or wilderness seasons, but He knows what is best, and you can trust Him as He leads you. Truthfully, I could not lead without the Holy Spirit's help. I am incapable of meeting all the demands and responsibilities placed upon me. God's supernatural presence continually sustains me. He is omniscient, omnipresent, and omnipotent. With the Holy Spirit living and abiding within you and alongside you, you will accomplish more than you ever dreamed.

Just ask Paul! The apostle and his companions were actively making plans, hoping to preach the gospel in Asia, but the Holy Spirit kept closing doors (Acts 16). First, they were kept by the

Spirit from preaching in the province of Asia. Then they tried to enter Bithynia, but the Spirit would not allow them. These were not missteps but divine redirections. Paul did not grow frustrated but remained sensitive to the Spirit's leading.

During the night, in the port city of Troas, Paul had a vision of a man of Macedonia standing and begging him, "Come over to Macedonia and help us" (Acts 16:9). Immediately, Paul and his team concluded that God had called them to preach the gospel there. That moment of spiritual clarity changed the course of human history. It opened the door for the gospel to enter Europe. The church in Philippi was established. Lydia was converted. A jailer and his entire household were saved. Revival resulted because Paul listened, adjusted, and obeyed.

That is Spirit-empowered leadership—being willing to reroute when God says no and being ready to move when He says go. What was the result? Europe was penetrated with the gospel, and Christianity expanded westward.

This is our testimony at ORU. The Holy Spirit is our secret, or maybe not-so-secret, weapon. Every year, the miraculous occurs—divine timing, supernatural provision, unexpected favor. That is the Holy Spirit at work. He leads, we follow, and He receives all the glory!

These six assets—a compelling vision, a practical plan, a committed team, a resource strategy, a strong resolve, and a powerful partner (the Holy Spirit)—are not merely concepts. They are the foundation of Spirit-empowered leadership. If you cultivate each of them, God will use you beyond what you have ever dreamed.

Leadership is not about control but calling. When God calls, He equips. When He equips, He provides. When He provides, He empowers. When He empowers, you are ready to lead.

CHAPTER 9

HIDDEN GEMS FOR LEADERS

Throughout the years, I have discovered that the most effective leaders possess quiet confidence, not built on charisma or hype but on deep, hidden principles. Let's explore four of these "hidden gems," or principles of leadership success. They are not flashy, and you will not find them trending on social media. However, if you want to lead with excellence over the long haul, these four insights will serve you well in your leadership journey.

1) HARD WORK AND DISCIPLINE

The first hidden gem of leadership is hard work and discipline. To lead well, you must work hard and practice significant self-discipline. Leadership is not given but forged, and the forge is often the grind of daily faithfulness.

Hard work may be the most underrated leadership attribute. I do not know a great leader who isn't also a great worker. The Bible teaches us that working diligently with discipline is a godly virtue. The writer of Proverbs points us to a hard worker in the animal kingdom as an example:

> Go to the ant, you sluggard; consider its ways and be wise! It has no commander, no overseer or ruler, yet it stores its provisions in summer and gathers its food at harvest. How long will you lie there, you sluggard? When will you get up from your sleep? A little sleep, a little slumber, a little folding of the hands to rest—and poverty will come on you like a thief and scarcity like an armed man.
>
> —PROVERBS 6:6–11

When I was in college, I had an 8:00 a.m. science class, and I was not a morning person. My bed and I had a great relationship, and it did not want to let me go each morning! I knew that if I was going to succeed, I had to develop discipline. One day while reading through Proverbs, I came across these verses about the ant and felt God's conviction. I was full of dreams and a desire to lead but struggling to even climb out of bed on time.

I began reading these scriptures and others on diligence every morning in my devotional time. Another scripture that spoke to me was "early will I seek thee" (Psalm 63:1, KJV). Over time I began a rhythm of discipline that shaped my life. Even now I am tempted to press the snooze button, but I continue to discipline myself to rise and begin the day and the work God has for me. Seeking Him first thing in the morning has made all the difference in my life and leadership.

The wisdom of the ant is to work hard, work together, and work while you can. These tiny creatures carry fifty times their body weight. They operate in colonies and have complex internal systems and controls without a leader in charge, and they achieve amazing feats! Ants are disciplined and work ahead to store for the future. They are a great example for us as leaders.

Leaders are formed through hard work.

Vince Lombardi said, "Leaders aren't born, they are made. And they are made just like anything else, through hard work. And that's the price we'll have to pay to achieve that goal, or any goal."[1] Leaders are formed through hard work. Usually you will discover leaders outwork their team members. You will not excel in leadership if you are lazy. Benjamin Franklin said, "The man who is good at making an excuse, is seldom good at anything else."[2] Discipline is the partner of hard work. It is what keeps us focused when distractions abound. Paul told Timothy, "Train yourself to be godly" (1 Timothy 4:7). Discipline builds spiritual muscle and momentum.

Work hard and be disciplined. Leadership begins with this hidden gem.

2) ATTITUDE

The second principle of successful leaders is attitude. Entitlement, pride, haughtiness, and resentment will hinder your leadership journey. Employers and teams want leaders with a great attitude. A bad attitude spreads like a virus and can infect an entire team with what I call a "staff infection."

Motivational speaker Zig Ziglar once said, "Your attitude, not your aptitude, will determine your altitude."[3] Viktor Frankl, who survived a Nazi concentration camp, famously said, "Everything can be taken from a man but one thing: the last of the human freedoms—to choose one's attitude in any given set of circumstances, to choose one's way."[4] Johnny Creasong commented, "Attitude is the voice of your heart! Attitude is the prophet of your future. It determines your destiny."[5]

> *Attitude is the prophet of your future.*
> *It determines your destiny.*

Your attitude prophesies your future. Attitude matters because it determines how you respond to people, pressure, and problems. Leaders set the tone and influence outcomes with their attitudes; a positive attitude leads to success. If you lead and serve joyfully, others will recognize the difference and be inspired. If your attitude is bitter, others will be discouraged and grow weary.

So ask yourself, "On a scale of one to ten, with ten as the most positive and joyful, how is my attitude today?"

3) SAVVY AND RESILIENCE

The twin gems of savvy and resilience form the third hidden gem. Savvy is spiritual and practical discernment—sharpness, perception, and the ability to make wise judgments in real time. Resilience is the strength to bounce back and to stay in the fight when the battle wears on.

The number one quality I look for when hiring a team member is spiritual savvy. This means they have godly determination and practical strategies to complete their job even when circumstances are challenging. They do not easily concede or accept defeat. They push through with grit and resolve. Leaders must have this quality. Leadership will punch you in the gut— people will disappoint you, and plans will fall through. That is when resilience and the ability to take a hit and keep moving matter. On the other side of the pain is victory. If you succumb to defeat too soon, you will never see what you are capable of or receive the reward.

Many times in my leadership I have felt discouraged and as if I could no longer continue. The pressure I was under was intense. I did not know how I possibly could do one more television show, deliver one more message, or make one more trip. In those moments, the Holy Spirit spoke to my spirit, encouraging me to persevere and not quit. Souls and spiritual transformations are on the other side of my obedience to God! When you find yourself in difficult situations, learn to stay on the court and play while you are injured, and keep serving when you don't feel that you have another ounce of energy or perseverance in you. Keep a smile on your face and a good attitude, and you will win for the glory of God.

I have seen leaders endure financial crises, personal losses, even betrayal, and yet remain faithful. That was not merely due to strength. They possessed savvy and resilience. The ones who persevere not only survive but also lead with depth and authority.

4) FAVOR

Finally, we come to the fourth hidden gem of leadership, which is favor. Favor comes from the Greek word *charis*, which is the same root word translated as "grace" in English. However, favor is more than grace. We all experience the grace needed for salvation: "For the grace of God has appeared that offers salvation to all people" (Titus 2:11). Favor is a special grace upon an individual—an invisible quality producing visible results. You do not earn favor, but it results from humility, obedience, and a heart aligned with God's heart.

> *God's grace is given to everyone, but favor is given to a few. When you have favor with God, you appear to be God's favorite.*

God's grace is given to everyone, but favor is given to a few. When you have favor with God, you appear to be God's favorite. God's favor is worth more than any amount of money. With favor, God's provision will come, and doors will open.

Joseph is one biblical example of someone who found favor. He had favor with his father, provoking his brothers' jealousy. When his brothers sold him into slavery, Joseph was taken to Egypt and placed in Potiphar's house. There he acquired favor and was put in charge of the household. But when Potiphar's wife lied about his character, he was thrown into prison. Yet even in prison, God elevated Joseph to a position of authority. Ultimately, he received favor with Pharaoh, being appointed the second-highest-ranking ruler in all of Egypt. God elevated Joseph, who was faithful, industrious, acquainted with dreams, and secure in his father's love.

David was also a man of favor. From a shepherd boy to becoming a king, he was marked by several great attributes. He had integrity, and even when he sinned, he repented sincerely. David was also a skillful man, whom God used in great ways. David demonstrated courage in the face of adversity, such as when facing the giant Goliath, and refused to retreat. David was loyal and demonstrated this loyalty to Saul even when Saul was disloyal to him. The shepherd king was patient; he waited for God's timing for promotion. These qualities positioned David for the favor from God that he experienced.

Esther, who was elevated from an orphan girl to queen of Persia, had favor. She was a person of simplicity, beauty, and great courage. She had learned from her cousin and guardian, Mordecai, to have a faith in God that was greater than the fear of man. Ultimately, her fasting, prayer, and courage helped her acquire favor with a pagan king.

Favor does not replace preparation but multiplies it. Again, we hear the wisdom of Proverbs, "Good people obtain favor from the Lord, but he condemns those who devise wicked schemes" (Proverbs 12:2). The wise writer also juxtaposes good judgment against unfaithfulness: "Good judgment wins favor, but the way of the unfaithful leads to their destruction" (Proverbs 13:15).

When leading, pray for God's wisdom: "A king delights in a wise servant, but a shameful servant arouses his fury" (Proverbs 14:35). If you have wisdom, you will find favor with others. We are even told that "Jesus grew in wisdom and stature, and in favor with God and man" (Luke 2:52). As you grow in favor with God, you will grow in favor with people. Focus first on your relationship with God and developing godly qualities, and other blessings will follow. "Wisdom's instruction is to fear the Lord, and humility comes before honor" (Proverbs 15:33).

As you grow in favor with Him, you will be spotlighted for others to see, and God will use you for His glory. "Humble yourselves, therefore, under God's mighty hand, that he may lift you up in due time" (1 Peter 5:6).

These four hidden gems—hard work and discipline, attitude, savvy with resilience, and favor—will help shape you into a leader God can trust. True Spirit-empowered leadership is not formed in the spotlight but in the secret places, quiet choices, and everyday faithfulness. So dig deeply, remain faithful, train your attitude, grow your spiritual savvy, and don't quit when times are tough, and you will walk in favor that only God can give.

CHAPTER 10

PRINCIPLES OF LEADERSHIP

Leadership is a sacred trust. Spirit-empowered leaders not only manage people but shape futures. Throughout the years, I have identified several key principles that have anchored my leadership and sustained my calling. Let's explore a few of the most important lessons I have learned.

FAT LEADERS

The team you choose is essential to the success of your leadership. When identifying potential leaders to join my team, I look for individuals with characteristics that align with the acronym FAT.

- **Faithful:** Is this person faithful? Are they reliable, consistent, and trustworthy? When I consider someone for my team, I check their social media, references, and the people with whom they are associated to discover if they are faithful.
- **Available:** Is this person ready and available to join the team? Are they dependable? Leaders must be willing to respond when needed, demonstrating a readiness to serve and lead.
- **Teachable:** Is this person willing to learn? No one will know everything about a job, but are they willing to grow and receive instruction? A leader with a teachable spirit accepts feedback, learns from experience, and stays open to correction.

Are you and your team FAT—faithful, available, and teachable? If so, you will lead well.

LIKABILITY AND RESPECTABILITY QUOTIENT

While character anchors a leader, connection and credibility fuel their influence. This is where likability and respectability originate. Every leader has a likability quotient and a respectability quotient. If people do not like you, they will not follow you, and if people do not respect you, they will not follow you. The most effective leaders balance both.

Every leader eventually faces a choice: to be liked or respected. While likability helps in building connections, respect is the foundation for lasting leadership. People may initially follow a leader that they like, but they will remain loyal to a leader they respect. If you are forced to choose, always prioritize respect over popularity.

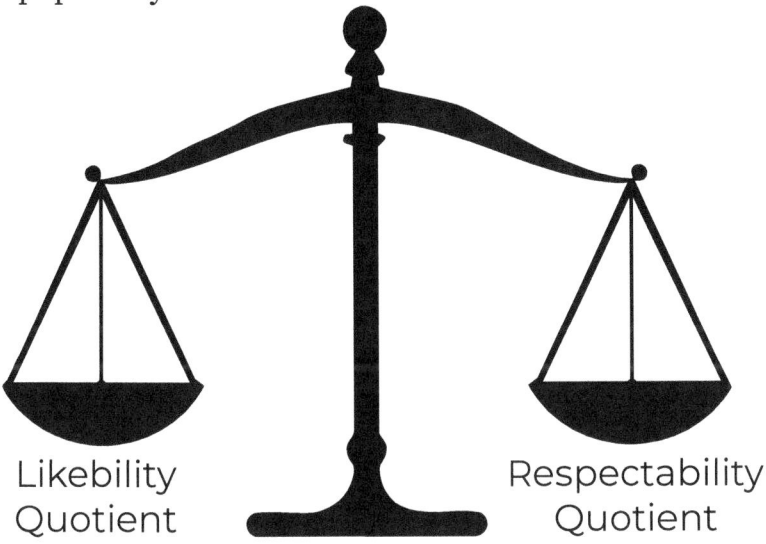

Likebility Quotient

Respectability Quotient

However, an imbalance in either direction can be problematic. A leader who is well-respected but not liked may struggle to inspire and connect with their team. On the other hand, a leader who is well-liked but not respected will lack the authority to make tough decisions. Leaders must work to develop both likability and respectability.

THREE INTELLIGENCES FOR LEADERSHIP

At ORU we emphasize three key intelligences that contribute to effective leadership: Intellectual Intelligence (IQ),

Emotional Intelligence (EQ), and Spiritual Intelligence (SQ). Having a balance of all three creates strong, well-rounded leadership.

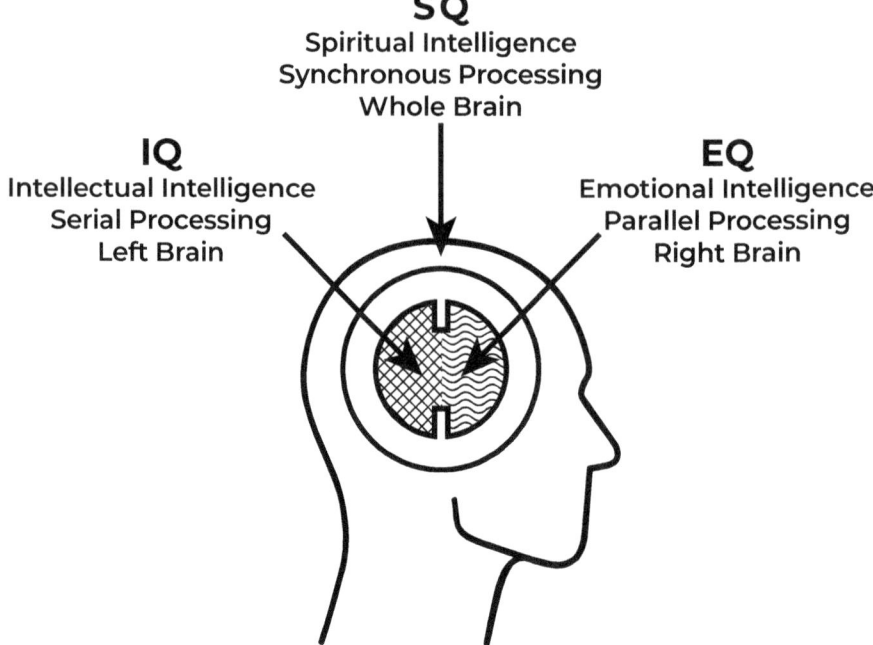

- **Intellectual Intelligence (IQ):** This refers to analytical ability, problem-solving skills, and knowledge of subject matter. Leaders must have a solid grasp of their field and the ability to process information effectively.
- **Emotional Intelligence (EQ):** EQ involves self-awareness, empathy, motivation, self-regulation, and social skills. Studies show that EQ is responsible for 58 percent of job performance and that 90 percent of top performers have a high EQ.[1] Leaders who cultivate emotional intelligence are more skilled at building relationships, managing teams, and navigating conflicts.

- **Spiritual Intelligence (SQ):** SQ is the ability to discern and align decisions with God's wisdom and purpose. Spirit-empowered leaders rely on the Holy Spirit for guidance, making decisions that reflect both wisdom and faith. Echoing words from the prophet Joel, Peter proclaims, "Your young men will see visions, your old men will dream dreams" (Acts 2:17). Leaders with a high SQ seek God's direction and operate with integrity and spiritual discernment.

When these three intelligences—IQ, EQ, and SQ—are developed simultaneously, leaders make better decisions. They know the facts, understand people, and lead with empowerment and wisdom from the Holy Spirit.

Momentarily reflect and ask yourself, "Which of these three intelligences is strongest in my life? Which needs to be developed the most?"

LEADERS ARE READERS

Another foundational principle of leadership is a commitment to lifelong learning. Leaders are readers. If you want to lead, you need to read. Learning from the experiences of great leaders is one of the most valuable ways to grow. During my ministry journey I have read numerous biographies and leadership books that have profoundly shaped my understanding of leadership.

Here are a few I highly recommend:

Biographies and Memoirs
- *Decision Points* by George W. Bush
- *John Adams* by David McCullough
- *Team of Rivals: The Political Genius of Abraham Lincoln* by Doris Kearns Goodwin
- *The Reagan Diaries* by Ronald Reagan
- *Presidents of War: The Epic Story, from 1807 to Modern Times* by Michael R. Beschloss
- *Oral Roberts: An American Life* by David Edwin Harrell Jr.

Leadership Theory and Practice
- *Leadership: Six Studies in World Strategy* by Henry Kissinger
- *Leadership: Theory and Practice* by Peter G. Northouse
- *Leadership: A Communication Perspective* by Craig E. Johnson and Michael Z. Hackman
- *Leadership Not by the Book: 12 Unconventional Principles to Drive Incredible Results* by David Green
- *Leaders: Myth and Reality* by General Stanley McChrystal
- *The 21 Irrefutable Laws of Leadership* by John C. Maxwell
- *The 360° Leader: Developing Your Influence from Anywhere in the Organization* by John C. Maxwell
- *The Five Dysfunctions of a Team: A Leadership Fable* by Patrick M. Lencioni

- *The 6 Types of Working Genius: A Better Way to Understand Your Gifts, Your Frustrations, and Your Team* by Patrick M. Lencioni
- *Leadership Pain: The Classroom for Growth* by Samuel R. Chand
- *Executive EQ: Emotional Intelligence in Leadership* by Robert Cooper and Ayman Sawaf
- *Executive Presence: The Missing Link Between Merit and Success* by Sylvia Ann Hewlett
- *5 Voices: How to Communicate Effectively* by Jeremie Kubicek and Steve Cockram

Spiritual Leadership
- *Spiritual Leadership: Moving People on God's Agenda* by Henry T. Blackaby and Richard Blackaby
- *Spiritual Leadership: Principles of Excellence for Every Believer* by J. Oswald Sanders
- *Leadership Prayers* by Richard Kriegbaum
- *The Leadership Lessons of Jesus: A Timeless Model for Today's Leaders* by Bob Briner and Ray Pritchard
- *The Jesus Style* by Gayle D. Erwin
- *The Making of a Leader: Recognizing the Lessons and Stages of Leadership Development* by J. Robert Clinton

As President John F. Kennedy said, "Leadership and learning are indispensable to each other."[2] This is why at

ORU we emphasize the importance of both intellectual and spiritual growth.

AREAS WHERE LEADERS ENCOUNTER TROUBLE

Leadership comes with challenges, and even great leaders can be ensnared in traps that hinder their effectiveness. Recognizing certain pitfalls will help us guard our integrity, effectiveness, and long-term influence.

> *Leaders jeopardize themselves when they stop pushing forward.*

Common areas where leaders face trouble are as follows:

1) **Maintenance Mode:** How do you handle your passion? Leaders jeopardize themselves when they stop pushing forward. The moment a leader settles into complacency and stops innovating, growing, or pursuing vision, decline begins. We see this when King David compromised and sinned with Bathsheba while he stayed home from battle (2 Samuel 11:1–2). Leaders must remain engaged, always seeking growth and momentum.

2) **Cutting Corners:** Do you always take shortcuts? Leaders who compromise in minor areas—cheating, exaggerating, or bending the truth—are positioning themselves for failure. Jesus said, "Whoever can be trusted with very little can also be trusted with much" (Luke 16:10). Cutting corners may bring short-term benefits, but this will ultimately erode trust and credibility.

3) **Entitlement:** Do you focus more on privilege than on responsibility? Leaders can be trapped in believing they deserve special privileges, but leadership is not about the perks. It is about responsibility. Leaders who focus on serving rather than being served will have a lasting influence.

4) **Sexual Sins:** Are you secretly fantasizing? Many leaders have fallen because they did not guard their hearts and control their thought life. Scripture warns, "Flee from sexual immorality" (1 Corinthians 6:18). Leaders must establish boundaries, accountability, and spiritual disciplines to protect themselves from temptation.

5) **Financial Impropriety:** Can God trust you with money? A lack of financial integrity can destroy a leader's credibility. Leaders must manage money with honesty and stewardship, remembering that "it is required that those who have been given a trust must prove faithful" (1 Corinthians 4:2). Tithing, generosity, and appropriate financial management are marks of a trustworthy leader.

I have learned many of these lessons firsthand. Early in my life and ministry, God taught me the importance of financial integrity. When I was in college, I was a poor student trying to find a way to make ends meet. I attended school on scholarships, loans, and grants. My mom and grandparents helped me with a car and occasional support, but they did not pay for my college tuition. I had to secure that on my own. One way I reduced my debt was by graduating in three years. Even then my student loans were not fully paid until seven years after graduation, but my degree was the best investment I ever made.

I secured various jobs and worked each semester to complete my schooling. During my last year in college Lisa and I were married, and although we were very much in love, we had very little in the way of financial resources. We lived in a trailer without underpinning, and during our first winter the pipes froze and burst, flooding the entire home. Today, we laugh about those days and cherish the memories, but at the time, we were simply broke newlyweds trying to make it through life.

Lisa worked at a department store and later secured a teaching job during my final semester before I began student teaching. After graduating, I was asked to do evangelistic work for a denomination in the state where I lived. They paid me $250 a month, plus offerings—our only source of income. We lived in a twelve-by-sixty-foot trailer and had occasional financial assistance from our parents.

When I traveled for evangelism, I would always tell Lisa, "Live low." She knew exactly what I meant. Our bank account was low, and we had to live within our means. I quickly learned that smaller churches often gave more generously than larger churches, and I relied on God's provision to meet our needs. The first church where I preached gave us an offering of about eighty dollars in coins. We were living by faith!

Two years into our marriage our son Ashley was born. Through it all God met our needs—not everything we wanted but everything we needed. When we reflect on those years, we see how blessed we were, even in the struggle.

In those early days I made a firm commitment that whether I made ten dollars or a thousand, I would always pay my tithes. The first 10 percent of everything we earned went to God, no exceptions or compromises. Beyond tithing, we also gave whatever the Holy Spirit led us to contribute. I remember pledging one thousand dollars to a building project at a campground, even though I didn't have the money at the time. I committed in faith, and within weeks God provided through unexpected offerings, allowing me to pay my pledge. It was a powerful lesson in trusting Him.

Nevertheless, living by faith was not only about giving; it was about stewardship. I paid my bills on time. I did not ignore my student loans or car payments. I was diligent in paying my electric, gas, and water bills. Through all of life's transitions—from pastoring to working in a parachurch ministry, from ministry roles to denominational leadership—God always provided. Amazingly, I have never missed a paycheck, even in seasons of major change.

You may ask, "What do tithes and financial stewardship have to do with leadership?" The answer is, "Everything!" Leadership starts with trust. Can God trust you? If you are faithful in handling what He gives you, whether little or much, He will entrust you with more.

> *If you are faithful in handling what He gives you, whether little or much, He will entrust you with more.*

At the end of a parable about a shrewd manager, Jesus stated the following:

> Whoever can be trusted with very little can also be trusted with much, and whoever is dishonest with very little will also be dishonest with much. So if you have not been trustworthy in handling worldly wealth, who will trust you with true riches? And if you have not been trustworthy with someone else's property, who will give you property of your own?
> —LUKE 16:10–12

If God can trust you with the physical resources He puts in your hands, then He can trust you with the great riches of His favor, blessings, and gifts. Although our stewardship involves money, it encompasses much more than money. God owns all and does not need our money. What He wants and needs before He can fully use us is our complete devotion. Money, being so critical to life, is one of the ways our commitment is regularly tested. Obey His principles, live generously, and the grace for leadership in your life will increase.

Avoiding these pitfalls requires vigilance, accountability, and a heart fully surrendered to God. Ultimately, leadership is about trust, humility, and faithfulness to the call of God on your life. By following these principles, you can lead well and finish strong.

CHAPTER 11

SPIRIT-EMPOWERED LEADERS AND THEIR MOVEMENT

Understanding who you are and how you fit into the world is critical to being a successful leader. As we discussed, knowing your physical family roots as a leader is important. Equally significant, or even more so, is understanding your spiritual roots. The Spirit-empowered movement has shaped the course of Christianity for more than a century, and as Spirit-empowered leaders, we are part of this movement. Briefly reviewing Christian history allows us to understand this movement and our spiritual roots. From the Protestant Reformation to the global Pentecostal and Charismatic awakenings, all are vital to comprehending our identity.

THE FOUNDATION OF THE SPIRIT-EMPOWERED MOVEMENT

The Spirit-empowered movement finds its deepest roots in first-century Christianity. We believe that the Holy Spirit, who fell on the day of Pentecost as recorded in Acts, is still actively working today. We also believe that Jesus' miracles, recorded in the gospel narratives, and the apostles' deeds, recorded by Luke in the Book of Acts, are still possible today. Jesus Christ and the Holy Spirit are the same yesterday, today, and forever. We accept the Bible literally and trust God to do what He did in the first century in the twenty-first century. These roots in the Gospels and Acts are the foundation of the Spirit-empowered movement. Even the Catholic Charismatic Renewal, which makes up 29 percent of the entire Spirit-empowered movement,[1] identifies its spiritual roots in the Acts of the Apostles.

However, it would be impossible to understand the Spirit-empowered movement without reflecting on Christian history and the many events that led up to the explosion of the Pentecostal and Charismatic renewals of the twentieth century. On October 31, 1517, Martin Luther, a Catholic monk, nailed his *Ninety-Five Theses* to the church door in Wittenberg, Germany, challenging the Catholic Church's sale of indulgences and, ultimately, its teachings on salvation and grace. The Catholicism of Luther's time taught that a person could inherit eternal life by their good works. During Luther's era, instances of religious corruption, such as the practice of selling indulgences to obtain or secure salvation for oneself or relatives, were prevalent.

Luther's protest and attempt to bring reform focused on three critical theological principles: salvation by grace alone (*sola gratia*), through faith alone (*sola fide*), and by Scripture alone (*sola scriptura*). Luther criticized the church for adding to the Bible and teaching man's decrees instead of God's. He declared that salvation is only by grace through faith and must be based solely on the Bible. Luther's teaching and bold courage formed the basis for Protestant Christianity.

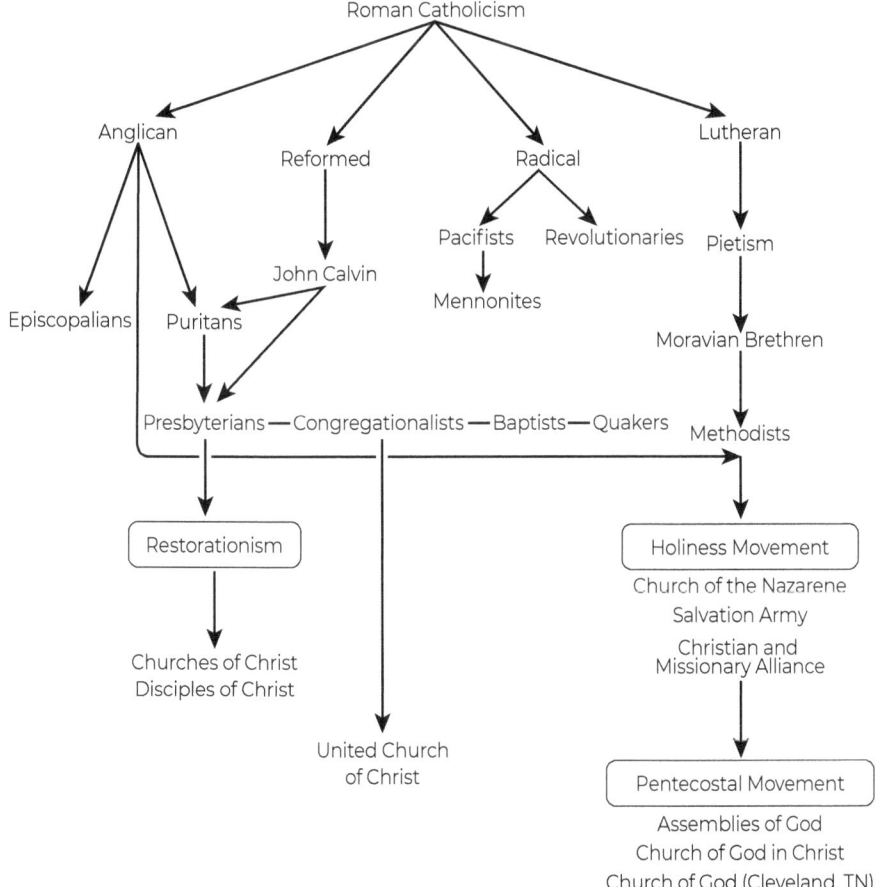

DEVELOPMENT OF PROTESTANTISM[2]

From this moment in history, the Protestant Reformation began. Since then it has evolved in many forms and undergone several minor renewals. This formed a diverse Protestant Christianity globally. This spiritual "family tree" will help you understand the history of Protestantism in more depth.

You will see we all came from Roman Catholicism in the West. If from the East, it would likely be Orthodox Christianity. Out of Luther's stand came the Lutheran denomination. After Luther the Protestant Reformation was born, placing great emphasis on aligning everything to the plain teachings of Scripture. John Calvin led the Reformation in Geneva and became one of the most influential figures, emphasizing the sovereignty of God. Some radical Reformers became revolutionary and even took up arms to fight the Roman Catholic Empire. Most, however, were pacifists, the biggest group being the Mennonites who sought separation from the state. Around this same time, Henry VIII sought separation from the Roman Catholic Church due to conflict with the pope over his divorce and formed the Church of England, or the Anglican church. While the King initially intended to have authority over this new denomination, the Reformation quickly gained momentum in England, fostering multiple dissenting movements.

One of these was Puritanism, which sought to align the Church of England more closely with Scripture and Calvinism. However, many of the Puritans fled to America to escape religious persecution. Puritans formed the Presbyterian and Congregationalist denominations, with early American ideals coming from Congregationalist churches. Later, American Presbyterianism was brought by Scottish and Scots-Irish immigrants who had experienced the Reformation under John Knox. Some Puritans began to emphasize believer's baptism and voluntary association, which led to the first Baptist denominations. After the American Revolution, the Church of England's expression in America became the Episcopal Church. Lastly, the Quakers in early America came from a separate dissenting group, the Society of Friends, led by George Fox, who had broken with Calvinistic teaching to seek direct encounters with God and were known for their "quaking" spiritual experience.

After American independence, freedom of religion opened the door for waves of revival and spiritual pursuit. The revival in Cane Ridge, Kentucky in 1801, for example, became a flashpoint of what would become known as the Second Great Awakening. On the left side of the tree, you see that one of the primary groups that emerged were known as Restorationists for their emphasis on restoring the church to the plain teachings of the New Testament. Today, these groups include Churches of Christ, Disciples of Christ, and United Church of Christ.

On the right side of the tree, however, is where the modern Spirit-empowered movement mostly originates, stemming from a movement among Lutherans known as Pietism and, eventually, the Moravian Brethren led by Count Zinzendorf in Central Europe. These believers, who were very sincere about their faith, along with the Puritans, formed the root of American Christianity. Out of the Moravians came the Wesleyan awakening. John Wesley was a member of the Church of England but was very influenced by the Moravian prayer and mission emphasis. Ultimately, those who followed Wesley broke away from the Anglican church and formed the Methodist church. Out of the Methodist church came the Holiness movement, and then a number of denominations were formed in the United States: Church of the Nazarene, Salvation Army, Christian and Missionary Alliance, and multitudes of other Holiness movements.

Following the Azusa Street revival, some of these groups became Pentecostal. If a movement accepted that tongues speech was evidence of Holy Spirit baptism for the believer, they were considered Pentecostal. These groups included Assemblies of God, Church of God in Christ, Church of God (Cleveland, Tennessee), International Pentecostal Holiness Church, the International Church of the Foursquare Gospel, and many others.

Protestantism is extremely diverse, with many global expressions. Some are very conservative, while others are less conservative. Some Protestants were influenced by the Holy Spirit and formed the Pentecostal movement. Though the Protestant Reformation leaned heavily on rationalism, the Spirit-empowered movement embraces both rationalism and mysticism, acknowledging the continued presence and power of the Holy Spirit, while also basing all Christian experience on Scripture.

THE FIRST GREAT AWAKENING

The First Great Awakening emerged in the 1730s among the Congregationalists, Puritans, and Pietists in the American colonies. This awakening was corollary to and fueled by the ministry of John Wesley and George Whitefield. One of the epicenters for this revival occurred in Northampton, Massachusetts, under the ministry of Jonathan Edwards.

Edwards, a pastor of a Congregational church in Northampton, and his wife began to seek God. She started having what he would call "swooning" or "emotional spells" in the presence of God.[3] Edwards began to preach very significant messages, including the most well-known sermon in American history, "Sinners in the Hands of an Angry God." After days of praying without eating or sleeping, Edwards preached this message. His heart's cry was, "God, give me New England!" While Edwards was preaching, it was reported that great conviction fell on the congregation. People began to cry and hung on to the pews in front of them so they would not fall into hell.[4]

Out of that moment, and many others like it, the First Great Awakening transpired. During this move of God's Spirit fifty thousand people were converted to Jesus Christ in a relatively unconverted and new world.[5] George Whitefield, a friend of Benjamin Franklin, was also instrumental in the First Great Awakening. Whereas Edwards would stand at a pulpit and read a text, Whitefield was more dramatic. He would incorporate illustrations, move his arms, and exhibit strong emotion. He had a booming voice, and Franklin calculated that Whitefield could preach to thirty thousand people without the use of a microphone.[6] People were touched dramatically and even fell under the power of God.[7] These revivals set the stage for future movements of God in the nation.

THE SECOND GREAT AWAKENING

The First Great Awakening played an integral role in establishing the first major spiritual revival and spread of the gospel in the American colonies. Many believe that it also gave the American colonists the moral courage for the American Revolution. Awakenings always result in social change. In this case the change involved the courage to stand against England and become an independent nation.

Nevertheless, after the First Great Awakening and the Revolutionary War, most scholars and sociologists deemed America spiritually bankrupt. Some said that one out of five colonists was an alcoholic, bank robberies were a daily occurrence in cities, women were afraid to go out at night, and not a single Christian student was found at Harvard University.[8] John Marshall, the Supreme Court Chief Justice of the United States, said the church was "too far gone to ever be redeemed."[9] The pervasive moral injury experienced during the Revolutionary War led to the nation's spiritual decline. Amid these bleak spiritual days a group of ministers began to unite with the express purpose of pursuing a spiritual turnaround in the nation. In the 1790s they called for prayer on the first Monday of every month nationwide.[10] These consistent prayer meetings formed the foundation for a fresh outpouring of the Spirit that would become known as the Second Great Awakening. The camp meetings of the early 1800s were an important aspect of the Second Great Awakening.

One of the first large camp meetings was the Cane Ridge Revival of 1801 near Lexington, Kentucky. The small frontier town had a population of less than two thousand in 1800.[11] However, more than twenty thousand people, which was ten times the population, gathered at this revival.[12] People came in wagons, on horseback, and on foot from several states to seek God together. Various denominations united at the Lord's table, and communion was the central focus of the resulting revival. At this time in the history of the church, people did not take Communion unless they were right with God, which urged attendees to embrace a spirit of repentance. At the Cane Ridge revival what some would call "holy chaos" ensued, becoming a precursor for the Holiness movement and the Pentecostal movement in the days ahead. The governor of Kentucky was touched and fell under the power of the Holy Spirit.[13] One Methodist preacher said, "I turned to go back and was near falling; the power of God was so strong upon me, I turned again and losing sight of the fear of man, I went through the house shouting and exhorting with all possible ecstasy and energy, and the floor was soon covered with the slain."[14]

Another witness during the revival recorded: "sinners dropping down on every hand, shrieking, groaning, crying for mercy, convoluted."[15] Additionally, reports were: "Professors praying, agonizing, feigning, falling down in distress for sinners or in raptures of joy! Some singing, some shouting, clapping their hands, hugging and even kissing, laughing; others talking to the distressed, to one another, or to opposers of the work, and all this at once."[16] These are just a few of the many accounts of what transpired during the revival. Paul

Conkin, late Vanderbilt University historian and author of *Cane Ridge: America's Pentecost,* said that the Cane Ridge Revival "arguably remains the most important religious gathering in all of American history, both for what it symbolized and the effects that flowed from it."[17]

After studying the Second Great Awakening, I tend to agree that this was one of the more significant religious gatherings in American history. What happened at Cane Ridge shook America for the good and changed the nation, but I believe that the global impact of the Azusa Street Revival has been greater. I have visited Cane Ridge several times, and the cabin where much of the revival took place is still on the grounds today. Undeniably, it is a fascinating place.

The effect of the Second Great Awakening on America should not be underestimated. While the First Great Awakening ignited courage for the Revolutionary War, the Second Great Awakening wrought several significant social changes in the nation. Most notably it helped broaden public education and gave Americans the spiritual courage to overthrow the scourge of slavery. The impact of these awakenings influenced abolitionism, public education, and social reform. Although Cane Ridge was one of the most notable of the camp meetings, other gatherings of believers occurred across the nation, forming a pattern for revival throughout the nineteenth century.

THE HOLINESS AND PENTECOSTAL MOVEMENTS

The nineteenth century witnessed the rise of the Holiness movement, which highlighted sanctification and the pursuit of holy living. A prominent leader at the time was Phoebe Palmer. Palmer emphasized that believers could experience entire sanctification—a deeper work of grace that purified the heart. John Wesley taught that sanctification is a process throughout a person's lifetime. Palmer and others like her believed that if a person could be holy someday, they could be made holy today. Phoebe taught that Jesus not only paid the price for us to be forgiven of our sins, but He paid the price for us to live without sin. This teaching was revolutionary as people began to seek and experience sanctification across America. Palmer's theology influenced the Nazarene denomination as well as other Holiness denominations.

Another prominent leader during the Holiness revival was Charles Finney, who began the practice of calling people to respond in what is now known as altar calls.[18] Before this time altar calls were not standard practice in church services like they are today. Finney began inviting people forward at the end of his messages to give their lives to Jesus or seek deeper blessings. This practice revolutionized revivalism and crusade evangelism.

During this time the Keswick movement emerged. While these leaders focused on sanctification, they did not believe in the shorter way that Phoebe Palmer taught; rather, they believed that everyone would have sin with them until they went to heaven. In other words, we could never be free from sin while on earth.[19] The Keswick movement heavily influenced what is now the Assemblies of God and its theology. Phoebe Palmer's teaching influenced other groups such as the Church of God in Christ, the Church of God, and the Pentecostal Holiness Church.

AZUSA STREET

At the turn of the twentieth century the Pentecostal movement emerged, ushering in a fresh understanding of baptism in the Holy Spirit with the evidence of speaking in tongues. Charles Fox Parham, the father of Pentecostalism, led a Bible school called Stone's Folly in Topeka, Kansas. Parham asked his students to study Scripture to determine the most common sign of receiving baptism in the Holy Spirit. As these mostly college-age students in the Bible school studied Scripture, they agreed that the most obvious answer to Parham's question was the experience of speaking in tongues. They recounted that tongues speech was the most repeated evidence of receiving the blessing of the baptism of the Holy Spirit after conversion. One of the students, Agnes Ozman, asked the others to pray for her to receive the gift of the Holy Spirit with the evidence of speaking in tongues.

On New Year's Day 1901, one hundred years after the Cane Ridge Revival in 1801, they prayed for Ozman, and she began to speak in tongues.[20] Parham recorded, "I laid my hand upon her head and prayed. I had scarcely repeated three dozen sentences when a glory fell upon her, a halo seemed to surround her head and face, and she began speaking in the Chinese language, and was unable to speak English for three days. When she tried to write in English to tell us of her experience, she wrote in Chinese, copies of which we still have in newspapers printed at that time."[21] Initially, when people received the baptism of the Holy Spirit, they thought they were speaking in a known tongue (*xenolalia*) rather than an unknown tongue (*glossolalia*).

Recognizing that believers throughout church history have recorded ecstatic speech or speaking in tongues is noteworthy.[22] The difference in Ozman's case and the teaching of Parham that would flow out of God's working is that people identified tongue speech as the evidence of being filled with or baptized in the Holy Spirit.

After this experience Charles Parham was forced to leave the city of Topeka. Parham decided to move his ministry school to Houston, Texas.[23] During the early 1900s Jim Crow laws forcing racial segregation were in effect in Houston. One of the rules was that a white teacher could not have a black student in their classroom. During Parham's school in Houston a black student sat in the hallway listening to Parham teaching on the third blessing of receiving the baptism of the Spirit. The young black student was partially blind and somewhat uneducated.[24] However, as he listened to Parham's teaching, he believed every word. The student's name was William Seymour.[25]

Seymour was soon called to pastor a small Holiness congregation in Los Angeles, California. He carried Parham's teachings on Holy Spirit baptism with him. When he preached on speaking in tongues and its relationship to the baptism of the Holy Spirit, the founding pastor was not happy and ultimately locked Seymour out of the building. The Holiness Church Association made the decision that he could no longer pastor this congregation.[26] After this incident members of the congregation who were touched by Seymour's ministry began joining his prayer meeting. As the prayer meeting grew, it was moved to a house on Bonnie Brae Street, where a group continued to gather. Seymour again began preaching his message on Spirit baptism. The small group that gathered began a ten-day fast, and as they fasted, some began to receive the blessing and speak in tongues, including Seymour himself. Revival erupted, and people from all over Los Angeles started coming to Bonnie Brae Street to receive their personal Pentecost.[27]

The house was so full that the porch used as a platform for preaching and leading fell through. Seymour and his flock ultimately moved to a building at 312 Azusa Street. It was a former church that had been used as a livery stable and endured an arson attack. They rented the building for the revival, cleaned the facility, hung lights from the low ceiling, added an assortment of old benches and chairs, and built a small wooden altar, platform, and benches for kneeling.[28] By April 18, 1906, the revival was going full speed at Azusa Street. That morning, an earthquake shook San Francisco, just four hundred miles to the north.[29] That very day, the *Los Angeles Daily Times* reported on the events at Azusa Street. In section B on page 1 of the newspaper was the heading "Weird Babel of Tongues. New Sect of Fanatics Is Breaking Loose. Wild Scene Last Night on Azusa Street. Gargle of Wordless Talk by a Sister."[30]

What happened at Azusa Street was unlike anything seen before. Worshippers of all races gathered in unity, experiencing prophecies, healings, and supernatural encounters. People would experience the power of the Holy Spirit and receive their personal Pentecost, marked by the evidence of speaking in tongues. People literally from around the world visited Azusa Street to experience this fresh outpouring of the Spirit. Azusa Street had five basic theological tenets: justification by faith, entire sanctification as an instant second blessing, baptism in the Holy Spirit with tongues as "Bible evidence,"

divine healing as in the atonement, and the second coming rapture. This revival was also marked by humility, holiness, harmony, harvest, and hunger.

Frank Bartleman, historian of the revival, said, "Proud, well-dressed preachers come in to 'investigate.' Soon their high looks are replaced with wonder. Then conviction comes, and very often you will find them in a short time wallowing on the dirt floor, asking God to forgive them and make them as little children."[31]

Bartleman also wrote, "The color line was washed away by the blood of Jesus Christ."[32] Another reporter said, "Disgraceful intermingling of the races. They cry and make howling noises all day and into the night. They run, jump, shake all over, shout to the top of their voice, spin around in circles, and fall out on the somewhat blanketed floor, jerking, kicking, and rolling all over it. Some of them pass out and do not move for hours as though they were dead."[33]

Hundreds of miracles were experienced at Azusa Street. It was as if heaven dropped a spiritual bomb in Los Angeles, and the fallout has continued for more than 120 years around the world!

THE FIRST, SECOND, AND THIRD WAVES

Azusa Street was a powerful revival, and many lives were revolutionized. This ushered in what is called the first wave of Spirit-empowered Christianity that gave rise to what are now known as the historic or classical Pentecostal denominations: Assemblies of God, Church of God, Pentecostal Holiness, Foursquare, Church of God in Christ, and many others.

The Spirit-empowered movement did not stop with historic Pentecostalism. In the mid-twentieth century a second wave—the Charismatic Renewal—swept through mainline Protestant and even Catholic churches. Oral Roberts, who was raised in a Pentecostal Holiness church, part of the historic Pentecostal movement, became one of the fathers of a new move of the Holy Spirit which was called the Charismatic Renewal. The emphasis of the movement was on prayer language, signs, wonders, healings, miracles, and seed faith. Dennis Bennett, the rector of St. Mark's Episcopal Church in Van Nuys, California, announced on Easter of 1960 that he had received the baptism of the Holy Spirit and spoke in other tongues.[34] Bennett did not immediately leave the denomination but began introducing the work of the Holy Spirit to Episcopalians.

During this same time, Oral Roberts was gaining prominence across America due to his television ministry and his ability to reach people in other denominations through his healing crusades. He utilized a new vocabulary in his ministry, including terms like prayer language, point of contact, and seed faith.

By the 1960s and '70s millions of Catholics, Lutherans, Baptists, and Episcopalians had received the baptism of the Holy Spirit, many remaining within their churches. Today, an estimated 192.5 million Charismatic Catholics have been filled with the Holy Spirit and operate in the gifts.[35]

In the first wave new denominations formed. In the second wave people stayed in their denomination and received the Holy Spirit. However, a third wave followed in the late twentieth century, characterized by nondenominational Spirit-empowered churches. These churches were known as neo-Pentecostal or neo-Charismatic. They were not connected to or under traditional denominations, many times forming "networks" of their own. They embraced signs, wonders, and Spirit-led ministry without formal denominational structures.

THE FUTURE OF THE SPIRIT-EMPOWERED MOVEMENT

Today, nearly seven hundred million Spirit-empowered believers worldwide span historic Pentecostals, Charismatics, and independent Spirit-filled movements.[36] The top nations embracing Spirit-empowered Christianity include Brazil, the United States, Nigeria, the Philippines, and China.[37] As we look ahead, a fourth wave of Spirit-empowered experiences appears to be rising, marked by digital evangelism, global connection, and hunger for God by a new generation.

What does this mean for Spirit-empowered leaders? It means we must steward revival well. History shows that moves of God can be messy, but they are also transformative. Like Luther, Edwards, Seymour, and Roberts, we must embrace both conviction and courage, knowing that the Holy Spirit is still moving today. I sense that today's young Spirit-empowered believers will initiate a fourth wave. Their spiritual hunger, coupled with technology and exposure to global connection, is going to allow us to see a fresh move of the Holy Spirit in the twenty-first century.[38]

Are you ready to be part of the next great awakening?

> *As we look ahead, a fourth wave of Spirit-empowered experiences appears to be rising, marked by digital evangelism, global connection, and hunger for God by a new generation.*

CHAPTER 12

HEALING IN LEADERSHIP

In the journey of Spirit-empowered leadership, understanding and applying the principles of healing is essential. Healing is not only a physical process but a spiritual one that transforms lives. As leaders, we are called to be conduits of God's healing power.

This chapter highlights ten foundational principles of healing that we can draw from biblical teaching and the ministry of Jesus. These principles will guide you in becoming a person of healing, equipped to bring God's restorative power to the marketplace, your ministry, your family, and wherever God calls you to lead.

Healing is a profound aspect of God's nature. As we delve into these principles, we will see how healing advances God's kingdom and brings Him glory. I have been healed many times and seen others healed as well, yet I do not know everything about healing. I do know that healing is from God, and His will is to heal.

By understanding and embracing these truths, you can become an effective instrument of healing, embodying the Spirit-empowered leadership that transforms lives and honors God.

PRINCIPLE 1: GOD IS A HEALING GOD.

God reveals Himself in the Bible as a healing God; one of His names is *Jehovah Rapha*, the God who heals. When the Israelites came to the bitter water in the wilderness, God spoke to them, promising healing to those who listened and obeyed His commands. Despite the presence of sickness and death due to the fall of Adam, God intervenes in the world to bring healing. Sickness and death entered through Adam's sin, but God's nature is to heal. We hear Him declare this to the Israelites in the wilderness when He reveals His name, *Yahweh Rapha*:

> If you listen carefully to the Lord your God and do what is right in his eyes, if you pay attention to his commands and keep all his decrees, I will not bring on you any of the diseases I brought on the Egyptians, for I am the Lord, who heals you.
>
> —EXODUS 15:26

PRINCIPLE 2: JESUS' EARTHLY MINISTRY WAS FILLED WITH HEALINGS.

Jesus' earthly ministry continually demonstrated God's heart to heal. Of the thirty-seven verified miracles in the New Testament, twenty-six were supernatural healings, including raising people from the dead. Jesus performed miracles such as turning water into wine, walking on water, and feeding five thousand from five loaves and two fish, but more than anything, He healed. He brought healing wherever He went.

In India, among a plethora of gods worshipped, Jesus is often recognized as the healing God. Jesus' ability to heal has drawn the world's attention to Himself. His healing ministry was profound, demonstrating God's compassion. Throughout His ministry Jesus reached the deepest hurt on earth, bringing healing to and profoundly touching hearts.

One of the reasons people are drawn to Jesus' healing power is that our health touches us deeper than anything else. When we are sick, we are deeply affected. When Satan attacked Job, he first attacked his finances, his resources, and even his family, but God would not let him touch Job's body in the first attack (Job 1:12). God, and even the devil, knew that health is very personal to us. Health is one of the greatest gifts of life. When Jesus brings healing, He is reaching to the core of humanity to bring restoration in a profoundly personal way.

PRINCIPLE 3: HEALING IS PROVIDED IN THE ATONEMENT.

> He was pierced for our transgressions, he was crushed for our iniquities; the punishment that brought us peace was on him, and by his wounds we are healed.
> —Isaiah 53:5

> "He himself bore our sins" in his body on the cross, so that we might die to sins and live for righteousness; "by his wounds you have been healed."
> —1 Peter 2:24

These Scriptures emphasize that Jesus' suffering and wounds bring healing. Jesus' sacrifice on the cross not only covers our sins but also provides healing for our bodies. He shed His blood, so our sins could be covered. He also gave His body so that we could be healed. Jesus bled from numerous places in His body, representing different aspects of healing. His head, hands, feet, face, back, and sides were all places of wounding. As Eve was taken from Adam's side, Jesus bled from His side to purchase the bride of Christ. Jesus especially bled from His back as the Romans punished Him with the cat-o'-nine-tails to emaciate Him before the cross.

Crucifixion was one of the cruelest forms of execution in history. It was bloody and painful. Jesus never sinned, but we did, and He willingly gave His life for us and bore the suffering to alleviate our sufferings. By His stripes we are healed!

By His stripes we are healed!

PRINCIPLE 4: THE HOLY SPIRIT CONTINUES CHRIST'S MINISTRY THROUGH US.

As Spirit-empowered leaders, we are called to continue Jesus' healing ministry in today's world. Following His crucifixion and resurrection, Jesus said to His disciples, "'Peace be with you! As the Father has sent me, I am sending you.' And with that he breathed on them and said, 'Receive the Holy Spirit'" (John 20:21–22). Jesus gave the power, which operated through Him, to His disciples. His commission was clear: "Jesus called his twelve disciples to him and gave them authority to drive out impure spirits and to heal every disease and sickness" (Matthew 10:1).

Two important words we identify in these passages in the original language are *exousia* and *dunamis*. The King James Version interprets both Greek words as the English word "power." Other translations delineate the two as they are in the original language. *Exousia* refers to authority, while *dunamis* refers to dynamic power.

The illustration of a police officer helps us understand the two types of power. A police badge gives the officer authority to use the power necessary to subdue. However, the officer also has a gun. If the badge is *exousia*, the gun is *dunamis*—real power to make something happen. As believers, we are called to be healers, and through Jesus, we have been given *exousia*, authority, over sickness and disease. The Holy Spirit is our *dunamis*—dynamic power to bring healing into effect.

PRINCIPLE 5: DEMONSTRATED FAITH ACCESSES HEALING.

How do we move from sickness to healing and accessing healing for others? Several occasions in Jesus' ministry show healing coming through faith demonstrated in action.

John records a story of Jesus' encounter with a man who was born blind. Jesus spat on the ground, made mud with His saliva, and put it on the man's eyes. He then instructed the man to wash in the Pool of Siloam. The blind man obeyed and was miraculously able to see (John 9:1–7). When the blind man moved through the streets of Siloam in raw obedience to Jesus, he was healed. His demonstrated faith positioned him for healing.

Luke records Jesus' healing of ten men with leprosy. They called out to Him, "Jesus, Master, have pity on us!" (Luke 17:13). Jesus then instructed them to show themselves to the priest. While they were on their way to the priest in obedience to Jesus' command, they were cleansed of their disease (v. 14).

Luke also shares the account of people who demonstrated faith for their friend's healing. The friends of a paralytic man tore open the roof and lowered him inside the house to where Jesus was. They knew that if they could get their friend into the presence of Jesus, he would be healed, and he was (Luke 5:18–25).

John wrote of Jesus' encounter with a man at the pool of Bethesda, who was unable to walk and said he had never been able to enter the healing waters. Jesus said to him, "Get up! Pick up your mat and walk" (John 5:8). This man, who had never walked before, obeyed Jesus' command and was healed.

Another account is of the woman with the issue of blood who pushed through the crowds with faith, saying in her heart, "If I just touch his clothes, I will be healed." Her active, demonstrated faith positioned her for healing. When she touched Jesus, "immediately her bleeding stopped and she felt in her body that she was freed from her suffering" (Mark 5:28–29).

Luke records the account of when Peter and John saw a lame man begging for alms at the temple gate called Beautiful while on their way to prayer. Peter said to him, "Silver or gold I do not have, but what I do have I give you. In the name of Jesus Christ of Nazareth, walk" (Acts 3:6) Peter helped the man to his feet, and he was instantly healed (v. 7). His faith demonstrated that Peter believed God is a God who heals. In the name of Jesus and through the power of the Holy Spirit this man was healed!

Oral Roberts was a man of faith and put that faith into action, seeing many men, women, and children healed by the power of God. Dr. Robert Fisher, who served as my predecessor at the Center for Spiritual Renewal in Cleveland, Tennessee, was a wonderful friend and mentor. As a young adult, Dr. Fisher was diagnosed with cancer in his foot and was told by doctors that it would need to be amputated. Believing God for healing,

Dr. Fisher attended one of Roberts' crusades and joined the prayer line. After explaining his condition, Roberts instructed him to stomp his foot. The first time, the pain was excruciating. Roberts asked, "That hurt, didn't it, son?" to which Dr. Fisher replied, "Yes, it did!" Roberts said, "Stomp it again." Though the pain was still great, each stomp hurt less than the one before. Two weeks later the cancer literally fell off Dr. Fisher's foot. He was completely healed![1]

> *You can access healing through the power of the Holy Spirit in Jesus' name if you believe!*

Repeatedly, we see this pattern of the word, obedience, and results. Healing is accessed by believing that what Jesus did on the cross through His sacrifice brought the power of healing into the world. You can access healing through the power of the Holy Spirit in Jesus' name if you believe!

PRINCIPLE 6: GOD USES MANY DIFFERENT METHODS FOR HEALING, INCLUDING MEDICINE.

My grandfather, M. E. Wilson, was a Pentecostal preacher who was a strict and austere man. One of his deep convictions was that believers should not take medicine but instead fully trust God for their healing. Early Pentecostal beliefs often rejected medicine, teaching that if healing was provided in the atonement, all we need to do is trust Jesus for healing and never take medicine. In 1960 my grandfather suffered a stroke while in the pulpit in West Virginia. For the next nine years of his life he could not walk or talk. During his sickness he never took any medication, not even an over-the-counter pain reliever. I honor my grandfather for being a man of conviction and living what he preached, but I do not believe his convictions on medicine were correct. God does use medicine and remedies to heal the human body. The story of Hezekiah verifies this understanding:

> In those days Hezekiah became ill and was at the point of death. The prophet Isaiah son of Amoz went to him and said, "This is what the LORD says: Put your house in order, because you are going to die; you will not recover." Hezekiah turned his face to the wall and prayed to the Lord, "Remember, LORD, how I have walked before you faithfully and with wholehearted devotion and have done what is good in your eyes." And Hezekiah wept bitterly. Before Isaiah had left the middle court, the word of the LORD came to him: "Go back and tell Hezekiah, the ruler of my people, 'This is what the LORD, the God of your father David, says: I have heard your prayer and seen your tears; I will heal you. On the third day from now you will go up to the temple of the LORD. I will add fifteen years to

your life. And I will deliver you and this city from the hand of the king of Assyria. I will defend this city for my sake and for the sake of my servant David.'" Then Isaiah said, "Prepare a poultice of figs." They did so and applied it to the boil, and he recovered.

—2 Kings 20:1–7

God heard Hezekiah's prayer and used a fig poultice as medicine to heal the king. In the New Testament, Luke, who was a physician, became one of Paul's closest companions. As they ministered, Paul was used by God to supernaturally heal the sick, while Luke assisted the sick in experiencing healing by physical means.

Oral Roberts' ministry exemplified the integration of prayer and medical science. From his healing and evangelistic ministry, he founded Oral Roberts University. At ORU he built The City of Faith, a hospital where people came for prayer and to obtain medical treatment. They combined medicine with prayer, demonstrating the belief that God uses both science and prayer to bring healing. At the front of ORU's campus is a statue of hands that many people call the "Praying Hands." These are actually known as "Healing Hands." One hand, which is slightly larger than the other, represents prayer, and the other represents science. This demonstrates how prayer and medicine, with an emphasis on prayer, come together to bring healing to God's people.

Scripture says, "Every good and perfect gift is from above, coming down from the Father of the heavenly lights, who does not change like shifting shadows" (James 1:17). God gave us science and uses it for our good. True science points us to the Creator, and God wants us to understand how the body works and bring healing to bodies through the best that science has to offer.

Medicine and prayer go hand in hand. Use medicine, a gift from God, and do not forget prayer. Remember that doctors are human, and they do not have all the answers. As it is said, they are practicing as physicians. They will not be perfect. The Great Physician is the one to whom we should turn for healing. Turn your heart to God, synergize medical treatment with prayer, and God will guide you to healing, even if it is with a fig poultice.

PRINCIPLE 7: HEALING INVOLVES MYSTERIES, AND GOD IS SOVEREIGN.

Healing is not always easily understood. God is sovereign, and His ways are sometimes mysterious. We must trust Him, knowing that He ultimately decides the outcome. Even the apostle Paul experienced this mystery. He was instrumental in helping multitudes of people experience healing; yet he wrote to Timothy, "Erastus stayed in Corinth, and I left Trophimus sick in Miletus" (2 Timothy 4:20). Paul understood healing involves mysteries because God is sovereign; He is not a machine. He may not always do what we want Him to do or explain His ways, but He is good, and we can trust Him.

I have experienced both being healed and not being healed. I have been supernaturally healed and healed through medicine. Years ago, I was coming out of the mountains after a time of praying and fasting for an international youth camp with the denomination I was serving. Following the camp was our general assembly, and I was intensely seeking God for His direction and help. During this time of study and prayer I consumed only water for several days. On the way down the mountain I decided to drink some apple juice. On the road back to the city my side started hurting. That night at home I was awakened at around two in the morning with severe, mind-boggling pain. It was so intense that I was pulling the carpet off the floor. Concerned, Lisa called prayer warrior friends to come to the house. They prayed for me that night, and finally said to Lisa that they thought I needed to be taken to the hospital.

When I arrived at the hospital, I could barely walk. The receptionist saw me and said, "Sir, you have a kidney stone!" I found out she was right. I was thankful for pain medication that night as the pain continued to intensify. The doctor ordered X-rays, and they gave me twenty-four hours to pass the stone before I had to go into surgery. I knew that if they did surgery, I would not attend the camp, which I was directing, and I would likely also miss the general assembly, where I was to be one of the keynote speakers. Determined to improve, I drank all the cranberry juice the hospital would give me, along with lots and lots of water. After wrestling with my condition and praying throughout the day to get better, I finally surrendered to the

Lord and prayed, "God, if you don't want me to lead this camp or preach at the general assembly, it's yours. I just give myself to you. I'm yours. If you will heal me, please do. But if you don't, it's OK. I love you, and I'm going to serve you through it all."

A short time after crying out that prayer to God, the same friends who earlier had been at my house praying came to the hospital. They prayed again as the hours were ticking away before my surgery deadline. The Holy Spirit filled the hospital room, and I climbed out of the hospital bed and began walking around the room, speaking in tongues, raising my hands, and praising the Lord. When I returned to bed, I still had my kidney stone. I knew that early the next morning, I was scheduled for surgery. However, I had peace. At about four in the morning, I experienced a breakthrough. I awakened with a different pain, and by the grace of God, I passed a large stone out of my body. Two days later, I flew to the camp and directed an amazing week of ministry. I also ministered at the general assembly under a strong anointing.

God healed me when I surrendered everything to Him. I have had other health battles in my life, and God has helped me in different ways. I was once diagnosed with lung cancer, and God immediately healed me. Another time, I experienced a 98 percent blockage in my heart and was close to a heart attack. God helped me through the power of medicine, and I had a stent put in to support my heart function. In that instance, God was still the healer, though He used doctors at Mayo Clinic. He works through different methods to bring healing into our lives.

PRINCIPLE 8: HEALING CAN BE PART OF SPIRITUAL WARFARE.

Prayer is crucial in spiritual warfare, especially when sickness is a direct attack from the enemy. While not all sickness is demonic, some instances require spiritual intervention through prayer. Spiritual warfare may involve battling against sickness through prayer and faith. When Satan's attack on Job went to the next level, the attack was on his body. "So Satan went out from the presence of the LORD and afflicted Job with painful sores from the soles of his feet to the crown of his head" (Job 2:7).

Satan can and does use sickness and disease to attack God's people. He attempts to discourage the believer and thwart the work of God. I have a young friend who was called as a missionary to northern India. Northern India is one of the most radically Hindu areas in the world, with numerous temples to a plethora of gods. My friend's calling and mission was to go to Northern India, enter the Hindu temples, and spend time there praying in the name of Jesus against the controlling demonic principalities in that region. My friend shared that multiple times after going to one of the temples to pray against the demonic powers, she would become sick with various ailments. She discovered that Satanic powers were affecting and afflicting her body.

In a less-direct fashion we can also witness the deterioration of health because of sin. Liver cirrhosis can be a result of alcoholism. Lung cancer can be a result of smoking; obesity, a result of gluttony; STDs, a result of sexual promiscuity; or other related issues and illnesses.

Sickness is a result of our fallen world, yet whatever the cause, Jesus is the healer and can rebuke Satan's power or even reverse the curse of sinful lifestyles.

PRINCIPLE 9: GOD SOMETIMES USES A POINT OF CONTACT.

Healing can be facilitated through a point of contact, such as laying hands on the sick or anointing with oil. The following scriptures emphasize the importance of these practices in bringing healing: "They will place their hands on sick people, and they will get well" (Mark 16:18). "Is anyone among you sick? Let them call the elders of the church to pray over them and anoint them with oil in the name of the Lord. And the prayer offered in faith will make the sick person well; the Lord will raise them up" (James 5:14–15).

Points of contact can serve as conduits for God's healing power. Your hands are meant to be a point of contact for healing, and when you lay hands on the sick, believe God that they will recover.

We read of this point of contact for the healing principle to occur in the apostle Paul's ministry. "God did extraordinary miracles through Paul, so that even handkerchiefs and aprons that had touched him were taken to the sick, and their illnesses were cured and the evil spirits left them" (Acts 19:11–12).

The cloths taken from Paul's body were a point of contact with the move of the Holy Spirit being experienced in Ephesus and the anointing on Paul's life. Faith connected with the source of God's power, and people were healed through this point of contact.

PRINCIPLE 10: HEALING HELPS ADVANCE GOD'S KINGDOM AND BRINGS GOD GLORY.

Healing is a taste of heaven on earth; it demonstrates God's kingdom and brings Him glory. When people are healed, it reveals the power of God in a fallen world and advances His kingdom. No sickness or disease is in heaven. Jesus taught us to pray, "Thy kingdom come, Thy will be done in earth, as it is in heaven" (Matthew 6:10, KJV).

> *As Spirit-empowered leaders, we are called to bring healing to the world.*

As Spirit-empowered leaders, we are called to bring healing to the world. By understanding and applying these principles, we can become instruments of God's healing power, advancing His kingdom and bringing glory to His name. Healing is a profound aspect of God's nature. The world and the workplace need healing, and we are called to carry the message of our healing and His power to that world.

CHAPTER 13

HANDLING FAILURE IN LEADERSHIP

One leadership lesson that every person, regardless of talent, passion, or anointing, must learn is what to do when things don't work, when your plan falls flat, when your dream breaks... What happens next if you fail in the attempt?

This section is not based on theory but on lived experiences. I have personally known the sting of failure. I have walked through moments where I felt the full weight of personal, professional, and spiritual defeat. Yet I have also seen what God can do with our lowest moments, if we allow Him.

Let's start with an important truth: Failing at something does not make you a failure. You may have made a mistake, but that mistake does not have to define who you are.

> *Failing at something does not make you a failure.*

THE REALITY OF FAILURE IN LEADERSHIP

Leadership involves risk, and with risk comes the possibility of failure. Zig Ziglar expressed this well: "Failure is a detour, not a dead-end street."[1] Failure is not the end of the road; it is merely a redirection. While you have breath, you have the opportunity for redemption.

Max Lucado expressed this concept even more poignantly: "God's book is written for failures. It is full of folks who were foul-ups and flops but got a second chance. Perfect people? No. Perfect messes? You bet. Yet God used them all. A welcome discovery of the Bible is this: God uses failures."[2] Joyce Meyer articulated this truth: "Failing at something does not make a person a failure. Most people who have done great things have failed many times before they actually succeeded."[3] We all fail, but what separates lasting leaders from the rest is how they respond in those critical moments. Bob Goff said:

> Failure is just part of the process, and it's not just okay; it's better than okay. God doesn't want failure to shut us down. God didn't make it a three-strikes-and-you're-out sort of thing. It's more about how God helps us dust ourselves off so that we can swing for the fences again. And all of this without keeping a meticulous record of our screw-ups.[4]

HANDLING FAILURE IN LEADERSHIP 175

History is filled with accounts of leaders who failed repeatedly but refused to quit.

Rory McIlroy, a world-class golfer, tried eleven times to complete the Grand Slam. He failed time after time, but he kept swinging. In 2025, he won the Masters Tournament, achieving the Grand Slam of golf by winning the US Open, the PGA Championship, the British Open, and finally the Masters.[5] I watched intently as Rory slipped on the green jacket, signifying his Masters championship and the completion of the Grand Slam, after eleven years of trying. I promise he was glad that he did not let the failures of those in between years stop him from trying.

In 1985 Steve Jobs was fired from Macintosh, the company he cofounded.[6] He made one of the greatest comebacks of all time, returning as the CEO of Apple in 1997.[7] Today, more than 2.2 billion people worldwide own an Apple device.[8]

One of the greatest inventors, Thomas Edison, said, "I have not failed ten thousand times. I've successfully found ten thousand ways that will not work."[9]

Theodor Seuss Geisel (Dr. Seuss) had his earliest manuscript rejected by twenty-seven publishers. Today, he remains one of the most beloved children's authors in history.[10]

Babe Ruth struck out 1,330 times but hit 714 home runs. He is known for his home runs![11]

Michael Jordan said, "I've missed more than nine thousand shots in my career. I've lost almost three hundred games. Twenty-six times, I've been trusted to take the game-winning shot and missed. I've failed over and over and over again in my life. And that is why I succeed."[12]

Finally, consider Abraham Lincoln—a masterclass in perseverance after failure. He lost more political races than he won, failed in business, suffered heartbreak, endured a breakdown, and yet persevered to become one of America's greatest presidents. His litany of failures is monumental.

- 1816: Lincoln's family moved from Kentucky to Indiana due to land disputes.[13]
- 1818: His mother, Nancy Hanks Lincoln, died of milk sickness.[14]
- 1828: His sister Sarah died during childbirth.[15]
- 1832: He lost his first campaign for the Illinois state legislature.[16]
- 1833: His general store business venture with a partner failed, leaving him with significant debt that took years to repay.[17]
- 1834: He ran for state legislature again and won.[18]
- 1835: Ann Rutledge, a close companion and likely sweetheart, died of typhoid fever, leaving him devastated.[19]
- 1836: He suffered a severe depressive episode, often described as a "nervous breakdown."[20]
- 1838: He lost his bid to become Speaker of the Illinois House.[21]
- 1843: He failed to secure the Whig nomination for US Congress.[22]
- 1846: He was elected to the US House of Representatives.[23]
- 1848: After serving one term in Congress, he was not re-nominated due to party rotation.[24]
- 1849: He was rejected for appointment as Commissioner of the General Land Office.[25]
- 1855: He ran for US Senate and lost to Lyman Trumbull.[26]

- 1856: He was considered for the Republican vice presidential nomination but received minimal support.[27]
- 1858: He lost the US Senate race to Stephen Douglas.[28]
- 1860: On November 6 he was elected as the sixteenth president of the United States, defeating three other candidates.[29]

Abraham Lincoln's resilience to persevere regardless of the odds or opposition prepared him for one of the most volatile and difficult presidencies in American history. Determination, even in the face of failure, forged in him the inner strength to successfully guide the nation through a civil war and into a new era.

Failing does not make you a failure. You only become a failure if you quit. Learn from these historymakers to keep going and try again.

WHAT TO ASK WHEN LEADERSHIP DOESN'T WORK AS PLANNED

When situations fall apart, good leaders ask the right questions:

1) **What were my motives?** Was this a God idea or just a good idea?
2) **Who was on my team?** Did I have the right people in the right roles?
3) **What was the environment?** Was this the right time and context?

4) **Where did we miss it?** What did I miss or misunderstand?
5) **What could or should I have done differently?** Where can I improve?
6) **What do I do now?** Do I try again, pivot, or wait?

MAXIMIZING FAILURE

If you fail, and you will, how do you maximize the failure?

- **Learn, learn, learn.** Everything in life is a learning experience. If you can learn from it, it is not a failure.
- **Document, document, document.** Record what happened. This will help you reflect on what could have been done differently and what you should or should not do in the future.
- **Consult, consult, consult.** Seek wise counsel and heed their advice. New sets of eyes may be able to see something you missed.
- **Decide on your next steps.** Determine whether to continue with the new insight and tools you have gained on the journey, wait for a better time, or punt. Move forward to God's next opportunity. When you fail, fail forward. Allow the moment to make you better, not bitter, and never ever quit.

I once led a denominational television ministry that completely collapsed under my watch. The failure was humiliating and painful. Feeling like a failure, I hoped to leave my position as communications minister. However, my mentor saw something that I did not. I was not finished.

> *When you fail, fail forward. Allow the moment to make you better, not bitter, and never ever quit.*

Instead, I was sent back to the same position, with no budget for television. I prayed and fasted for twenty-one days. On the second day of the fast God gave me a fresh vision and direction along with several steps to take. In obedience to what God implanted in my heart, I sought a man who had walked a similar road and asked him to be my coach. After my failure came obedience, and something remarkable was produced. The denomination permitted me to return to television with a small grant. I was determined, with God's help, to make this work. I proposed the idea for a program called *World Impact*, now known as *World Impact with Dr. Billy Wilson*. Thirty years later *World Impact* is broadcast in more than 150 countries and is available to approximately nine hundred million households each week. This accomplishment would not have happened if I had not failed first. God can use your greatest failure as the soil for your greatest fruit. Don't quit. God has something better in mind!

WHEN A LEADER FAILS MORALLY

Now let's examine an even more difficult matter. What happens when a leader does not fail in strategy but fails morally?

The Bible is full of such stories:

- **Samson:** Undone by lust, restored by grace, Samson repeatedly allowed his lust and impulsive decisions to undermine his calling. His entanglement with Delilah was the climax of a pattern of unchecked appetites. She eventually betrayed him, leading to the loss of his strength, sight, and freedom. Yet the story does not end in shame. In prison, Samson's hair—a symbol of his Nazarite commitment to God—began to grow again. More importantly, so did his dependence on the Lord. In his final act Samson prayed one last time for strength. God answered him, and Samson brought down the temple on the Philistines, defeating more enemies in his death than in his life (Judges 16:28–30).
- **David:** King David, Israel's greatest king, was a man after God's own heart, but he was also a man capable of great sin. His lust for Bathsheba led to adultery, deceit, and ultimately murder when he arranged for her husband, Uriah, to be killed in battle. David tried to cover his sin until the prophet Nathan confronted him, saying, "You are the man!" (2 Samuel 12:7). Faced with his failure, David did not make excuses. He broke. He repented. His raw cry of a shattered leader longing for restoration is recorded in Psalm 51.

HANDLING FAILURE IN LEADERSHIP

> Have mercy on me, O God, according to your unfailing love; according to your great compassion blot out my transgressions. Wash away all my iniquity and cleanse me from my sin. For I know my transgressions, and my sin is always before me. Against you, you only, have I sinned and done what is evil in your sight; so you are right in your verdict and justified when you judge. Surely I was sinful at birth, sinful from the time my mother conceived me. Yet you desired faithfulness even in the womb; you taught me wisdom in that secret place. Cleanse me with hyssop, and I will be clean; wash me, and I will be whiter than snow. Let me hear joy and gladness; let the bones you have crushed rejoice. Hide your face from my sins and blot out all my iniquity. Create in me a pure heart, O God, and renew a steadfast spirit within me.
> —PSALM 51:1–10

David was broken because of his sins. God forgave him, though consequences remained. Despite his failure, David remained a central figure in God's redemptive story.

- **Peter:** Despite his bold promises to stand by Jesus, Peter denied knowing Him, not once but three times, on the night of Jesus' arrest. The Gospel of Luke relates that after the third denial, Jesus turned and looked at Peter (Luke 22:61). Overwhelmed with shame, Peter wept bitterly (Luke 22:62). Thankfully, Jesus did not leave Peter in his failure. After the resurrection, in a quiet moment on the Galilean shore, Jesus reinstated Peter by asking him three times, "Do you love me?" With each confession of love, Jesus commissioned him again: "Feed my sheep" (John 21). Just weeks later, Peter stood boldly on the day of Pentecost, preached the gospel, and witnessed three thousand people receive his word and be added to the believers (Acts 2:14–41). This bold, Pentecostal preacher had experienced spiritual failure only fifty days earlier.

When a leader—or any believer—fails spiritually, the path back begins with three things:

1) **Embrace Repentance**—Real repentance involves owning your mistake, mourning over it, and then turning from it.
2) **Discipline**—God disciplines those He loves (Hebrews 12:6). It is painful but redemptive.
3) **Accountability**—You must walk with others who will ask the hard questions and hold you to a higher standard.

AVOIDING MORAL FAILURE

Moral failure is not inevitable. You can avoid it. Here are some steps on how:

1) **Stay Vigilant**—Peter warns us that the enemy "prowls around like a roaring lion looking for someone to devour" (1 Peter 5:8). That means you. Don't coast. Do not relax your guard. The devil doesn't take sabbaticals.
2) **Walk in the Spirit**—Paul exhorts the Galatian believers to "walk by the Spirit, and you will not gratify the desires of the flesh" (Galatians 5:16). The best defense is a strong offense. Pray. Fast. Be active in your faith.
3) **Be Healed**—Unresolved and unhealed wounds are open doors to the enemy. In the Old Testament, Baal-Zebub was the "lord of the flies" (2 Kings 1). Flies are drawn to wounds, and so are demons. Heal the wound, and the flies disappear. Many people carry wounds from abuse, rejection, or trauma. Satan uses those wounds to keep us trapped in shame, lust, and fear. When you are healed spiritually and emotionally, Satan's door of entry into your mind and heart is closed. Freedom is experienced, and restoration is the result.
4) **Maintain Healthy Relationships**—Healthy romantic and spiritual relationships protect us. The Bible warns us, "To avoid fornication, let every man have his own wife" (1 Corinthians 7:2, KJV). Intimacy without a covenant invites chaos.
5) **Become Accountable**—Who is asking you the hard questions? Who has permission to keep you accountable—open and honest? If no one does, you are vulnerable. Accountability helps you from secretly slipping. Find someone or some group to whom you are fully accountable.

MONITORING YOUR LEADERSHIP GAUGES

Before his own failure, Bill Hybels once taught about the three gauges in a leader's life:

1) **Physical**—Are you sleeping? Resting? Eating well?
2) **Spiritual**—Are you reading and meditating on Scripture? Praying? Hearing God's voice?
3) **Emotional**—Are you depleted? Drained? Disconnected?[30]

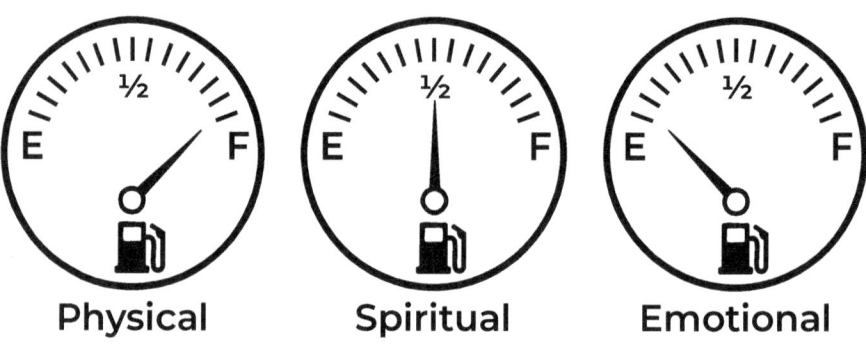

If you neglect any one of these, you are positioning yourself for collapse. You may need counseling—or you may only need a nap!

Essentially, leaders need to discover what restores them emotionally. I am convinced that many leaders fail simply because they are depleted emotionally and vulnerable to emotional triggers. What replenishes you emotionally and fills your emotional gauge? For me, solitude is one thing that replenishes my emotional tank. By nature I am an introvert who has been placed in an extroverted environment due to my many leadership responsibilities. However, interacting with people can emotionally drain me, so I must find time alone to reflect, pray, and rest. Every summer I spend at least two weeks in solitude. I avoid social media and disconnect (as much as possible) from human interaction. This time is used for prayer and reflection. Each year these two weeks are as valuable as gold for my leadership journey. I am refilled and ready to lead for another year as university president. However, I will still require moments during the year when I can withdraw to be alone to hear from God, replenishing my emotions. For others—especially extroverts—relationships replenish their emotional tank. And for others, nature, shopping, or exercising may be what fuels them. You need to discover what refills your emotional tank and stay emotionally strong.

HE IS ABLE

Remember that you are not alone. The New Testament writer Jude ascribes glory, majesty, dominion, and authority, "To him [God] who is able to keep you from falling and to present you before His glorious presence without fault and with great joy—to the only God our Savior, be glory, majesty, power and authority, through Jesus Christ our Lord" (Jude 1:24–25). He can keep you. Even when you fail, He is faithful. You are not your worst moment! You are God's child. Stand, regroup, dust yourself off, learn from your mistakes, and lead again.

CHAPTER 14

BECOMING A WHOLE LEADER

What does a Spirit-empowered leader look like in the twenty-first century? At ORU our mission statement is "to develop Holy Spirit-empowered leaders through whole-person education to impact the world." We have identified five outcomes that we believe every person needs to be a leader in our day. While these outcomes are part of our educational journey at ORU, they apply to anyone who desires to be a leader filled with the Holy Spirit. Leadership is not merely about gifting but includes being called by God and shaped by His presence. Spirit-empowered leadership means living a life of integrity, resilience, wisdom, global awareness, and bold vision. God is not only interested in what we do for Him but in who we are as we obey, serve, and lead.

To be a Spirit-empowered leader, we must develop holistically. In this final chapter we explore five key dimensions of that wholeness. Let's examine each of these leadership traits and how they shape a whole, Spirit-empowered leader prepared to lead in the twenty-first century.

1) SPIRITUAL INTEGRITY

This is where successful leadership begins. If you are not authentically walking with God, everything else will eventually collapse. Once again, the wise writer of Proverbs warns us: "The unfaithful are destroyed by their duplicity" (Proverbs 11:3). Integrity is derived from the root word integer and means "whole" or "complete" (e.g., a whole number versus a fraction). Spiritual integrity is living a life without duplicity or division, or fractional living. Duplicity would be to live one way in public and another way in private. Integrity influences all areas of our lives, encouraging us to live authentically for Christ.

> ***Integrity influences all areas of our lives, encouraging us to live authentically for Christ.***

When you have integrity, you do what you say you will do. You tell the truth. You're on time. You are faithful, dependable, honest, authentic, and sound at the core. Brian Tracy said, "Integrity is the most valuable and respected quality of leadership. Always keep your word."[1] Warren Buffett echoed this wisdom: "It takes twenty years to build a reputation and five minutes to ruin it. If you think about that, you'll do things differently."[2]

The legendary basketball coach John Wooden said, "Be more concerned with your character than your reputation. Because your character is what you really are, while your reputation is merely what others think you are."[3]

Integrity does not mean perfection, but it does mean congruence. Who you are in private is who you are in public. That is the kind of leadership that lasts.

2) PERSONAL RESILIENCE

How far can you be stretched without breaking? Resilience comes from the Latin word meaning "to bounce back," like a rubber band that is pliable and stretchable. Resilience is the quality of someone who has been knocked down but refuses to stay down. It demonstrates strength in adversity. Leaders must develop resilience to endure the ups and downs of life without losing their center.

In leadership you must minimize the highs and lows. Jesus taught that John the Baptist's ministry was to level the mountains, raise the valleys, and make the crooked paths straight (Luke 3:5). The Christian life brings the mountains down—you are not too emotionally high. It brings the valleys up—you do not become too emotionally low. True Christianity makes the crooked way straight. Leaders walk a "plain path," not ruled by emotions but by faith and consistency. Of course, you have time for celebration, but you must remain sober about the reality of life on earth. The resilient leader keeps going even when life is tough.

3) INTELLECTUAL PURSUIT

Knowledge is exploding. At one time centuries were required to double the world's knowledge base, but now it doubles in hours. In 1900 the world's knowledge doubled every four hundred years. If you knew something, you could depend on it to remain stable and consistent for the rest of your life. By 1950 the world was progressing at a faster pace, and knowledge was doubling every twenty years. By 1980 the knowledge base was doubling approximately every ten years. With the advent of the computer age, by 2000 this rate accelerated to double every eight years. In 2017 knowledge doubled every thirteen months, and today, experts estimate that knowledge doubles every twelve hours or less.[4] Due to advancements in technology and the flattened world, knowledge abounds and expands rapidly. Daniel prophesied that in the last days, "Knowledge shall be increased" (Daniel 12:4, KJV). This has indeed come true. Knowledge has not only increased but is exploding exponentially. By the time you finish reading this book, the knowledge base of the world will have already expanded significantly.

What is the implication of the knowledge explosion of our day? If you stop learning, you will fall behind. By 2030 an estimated 59 percent of the global workforce will require reskilling or upskilling.[5] Christian leaders cannot afford to be mentally passive. We are called to love God with all our heart, soul, *and mind* (Mark 12:30). Lifelong learning is a nonnegotiable for Spirit-empowered leaders.

> *Lifelong learning is a nonnegotiable for Spirit-empowered leaders.*

I remember recently walking into a biology class. I majored in biology in the late 1970s, but listening to today's students discuss cellular structure, I realized I only understood a tenth of what they were talking about. The field of cellular studies and biology has advanced that much. The majority of what I learned close to fifty years ago is now almost obsolete.

So we do not merely want to acquire facts—we want to pursue truth, fall in love with learning, and remain curious throughout our lifetime. Never settle or think you have learned everything.

One summer after my freshman year in college I returned home full of new knowledge and a little too much confidence. I was proud to be my family's sole college student and had learned so much. One night at the dinner table, my grandfather leaned across the table and said, "Boy, if you go to school another year, you're going to know it all." His gentle rebuke reminded me how little I truly knew. During my senior year at Western Kentucky University, I remember standing in the university's library, looking at the vast number of volumes and realizing I had probably only read one shelf of books. Even those eight stories in Western's library were a tiny sliver of the world's knowledge in the 1980s. Even more so now with the expansive knowledge bombarding us every day, we know extremely little compared to the totality of knowledge available to us. Humility keeps us hungry. We must remain students for life. Learning how to learn is a critical life skill in the twenty-first century. Pursue knowledge for the rest of your life. Leaders are always learning!

4) GLOBAL ENGAGEMENT

We live in a globally connected world unlike ever before. With technology a leader in Texas can connect with a pastor in Kenya or a business partner in South Korea in real time. I regularly participate in Zoom meetings with global leaders as part of Empowered21, the Pentecostal World Fellowship, or initiatives at Oral Roberts University. This type of connection was unimaginable just a few decades ago. When I was young, the only way I could have done this would have been to make a VHS tape and mail it via "snail" mail. In my lifetime we have developed the ability to connect face-to-face, across borders, in real time through technology. If I were not so busy preparing for my next Zoom call, this explosion of global connections would blow my mind!

In today's global youth culture, young people around the world listen to the same music, watch the same videos, and admire many of the same influencers through shared media. People are not as geographically bound as they were only one generation ago. That means when Generation Z gathers from across the nations, they already have common ground.

Leaders must be global citizens. The Great Commission is a worldwide mandate, and the gospel knows no borders. God's heart is for everyone in every corner of the world. John

Wesley once said, "I look upon all the world as my parish."[6] That is the kind of global vision every Spirit-empowered leader should carry.

5) BOLD VISION

If we serve the God of the universe, why would we dream small?

Oral Roberts had a sign on his desk at the university that said, "Make no little plans here." He only wanted people to bring big plans and dreams to him. When I became president of ORU, my former staff in Cleveland, Tennessee, bought me bookends inscribed with "Make no little plans here." They remain on my desk today. Spirit-empowered leaders are bold thinkers. We not only manage what is, but we also imagine what could be. What is your leadership dream? What is gestating in your heart? We listen to God, write down the vision, and run with it (Habakkuk 2:2).

Something powerful occurs when we write a God-given dream on paper. It becomes tangible. Trackable. Shareable. Vision gives direction, and direction gives people hope.

Our world is full of problems. God is mobilizing and engaging leaders with bold solutions—rooted in truth, bathed in prayer, and empowered by His Spirit.

CONCLUSION

A SPIRIT-EMPOWERED LEADER: THE FULL PICTURE

Reflecting on what you have read in these pages, how would you describe a Spirit-empowered leader? Here's a working definition:

> *A Spirit-empowered leader is a person empowered by the Holy Spirit to serve others by leading them and turning vision into reality, influencing them to cooperate in reaching a worthy goal.*

The Holy Spirit is a difference maker in leadership. He gives us:

- Supernatural insight
- Extraordinary wisdom
- Spiritual authority
- Notable integrity
- Personal giftedness
- Exceptional courage
- Exemplary resilience
- Astonishing love

These gifts and attributes transform potential into purpose, developing a holistic leader empowered to lead and change the world. You must be reliant on the Holy Spirit for successful leadership in whatever sphere of influence to which you are called. The apostle Paul wrote, "Not that we are competent in ourselves to claim anything for ourselves, but our competence comes from God" (2 Corinthians 3:5). This is surely my story too.

MORE THAN YOU CAN DREAM

A few years ago I drove on a country road past the small house where I grew up in Kentucky. My father left when I was five years old, and I was raised by my grandparents in a modest home across the road from a rough bar or "beer joint," as we called it. I fished in the lake beside the house most days every summer, rode my horse, played pool in the tavern across the street, and lived in a small town that was extremely spiritually dark.

As I sat that day in my car looking at the house of my childhood, I asked God, "How did this happen? How did a broken, sinful kid go from here to preaching the gospel around the world and leading a global university?" Truthfully, I said, "God, this is impossible. It makes no sense. How did You even find me here?"

The answer came gently and clearly. The Holy Spirit whispered to me, "It was Me, Billy. My eye was on you. My hand was on you. I knew where you were the whole time. I was just waiting for you to know Me." I drove away that day, reminded once again that it is "'not by might nor by power, but by my Spirit,' says the LORD Almighty" (Zechariah 4:6). Only God could have taken me from that dark community and sent me around the world for His kingdom. Only the Holy Spirit could have taken my broken pieces, made me whole, and empowered me to serve the many people I lead every day.

You may wonder, "How could God ever use me?" You may come from a situation worse than mine. Maybe you come from a neighborhood wrecked by sin, drugs, and failure. Perhaps you are from suburbia, which appears good on the surface, but behind closed doors, it is filled with sin and corruption. You may have come from a seemingly wonderful church on the outside, but it is full of hidden abuse. If you gain nothing else from this book, hear this: The Holy Spirit is your answer. At sixteen, when I was saved and baptized in the Holy Spirit, God exchanged His beauty for my ashes. He found me. He saved me.

He filled me. He healed me. He anointed me. He led me and made something out of me that I could never have dreamed.

> *The Holy Spirit is your answer.*

If you allow Him, He will do the same for you.

You may feel broken, unknown, or unqualified, but if you yield to the Holy Spirit, He will take your life and do something greater than you can imagine.

Do not waste your potential on foolishness and small thinking! Be whole. Be filled. Be bold. Be led. You will become more than you could ever have dreamed of by the power of the Holy Spirit. You will change the world as you are *Empowered to Lead*.

NOTES

CHAPTER 1

1. Thomas Carlyle, *On Heroes, Hero-Worship, and the Heroic in History* (1841), Project Gutenberg, https://www.gutenberg.org/files/1091/1091-h/1091-h.htm.
2. Peter G. Northouse, *Leadership: Theory and Practice*, 9th ed. (Los Angeles: SAGE Publications, 2022), 27.
3. Marjan Boerma et al., "Point/Counterpoint: Are Outstanding Leaders Born or Made?" *American Journal of Pharmaceutical Education* 81, no. 3 (2017): 58, https://doi.org/10.5688/ajpe81358.
4. Peter Drucker, *Managing for the Future* (New York: Routledge, 2013), 103.
5. Kevin Kruse, "What Is Leadership?" *Forbes*, April 9, 2013, https://www.forbes.com/sites/kevinkruse/2013/04/09/what-is-leadership/.
6. Warren G. Bennis, "Leadership Is the Capacity to Translate Vision into Reality," *Journal of Property Management* 73, no. 5 (September–October 2008): 13, https://link.gale.com/apps/doc/A186442346/AONE?u=googlescholar&sid=bookmark-AONE&xid=01a69393.
7. John C. Maxwell, "Your Influence Inventory," *Maxwell Leadership*

Podcast, April 17, 2019, https://www.maxwellleadership.com/podcast/your-influence-inventory/.

8. Murray Johannsen, quoted in Cindy C. Chojnacky, "Leadership Impact on Forest Service Operations: Intriguing Ideas from Public Administration Theories," *Journal of Forestry* 110, no. 8 (2012): 457–62, https://doi.org/10.5849/jof.12-023.

9. United States Air Force, *Air Force Doctrine Document 1-1: Leadership and Force Development* (Washington, DC: Department of the Air Force, 2006), https://www.safia.hq.af.mil/Portals/72/documents/AFD-070904-027.pdf?ver=2016-08-03-102920-717.

10. Clayborne Carson, ed., *The Autobiography of Martin Luther King, Jr.* (New York: Grand Central Publishing, 2001).

11. Dwight D. Eisenhower, "Quotes," Eisenhower Presidential Library, accessed August 14, 2025, https://www.eisenhowerlibrary.gov/eisenhowers/quotes.

12. Theodore Roosevelt, "Citizenship in a Republic," speech, Sorbonne, Paris, April 23, 1910, https://worldfuturefund.org/Documents/maninarena.htm.

13. Peter G. Northouse, *Leadership: Theory and Practice*, 9th ed. (Los Angeles: SAGE Publications, 2022), 27.

14. Northouse, *Leadership: Theory and Practice,* 84.

15. Northouse, *Leadership: Theory and Practice,* 109.

16. Northouse, *Leadership: Theory and Practice,* 185.

17. Northouse, *Leadership: Theory and Practice,* 253.

CHAPTER 2

1. Iyanla Vanzant, in Oprah Winfrey, *The Path Made Clear: Discovering Your Life's Direction and Purpose* (New York: Flatiron Books, 2019), 87.

2. Jonathan Swift, Thomas Sheridan, and John Nichols, *The Works of the Rev. Jonathan Swift, D.D.: With Notes, Historical and Critical* (New York: W. Durell, 1812).
3. Empowered21, "About Us," Empowered21, accessed September 30, 2025, https://empowered21.com/about/.
4. Billy Wilson, *The Power of One: Reaching Every Person on Earth* (ORU Press, 2023).
5. Walt Disney, "If you can dream it, you can do it," attributed quote, Goodreads, accessed August 14, 2025, https://www.goodreads.com/quotes/24673-if-you-can-dream-it-you-can-do-it-always *Note: This quote is commonly attributed to Walt Disney but has not been verified through primary sources.*
6. Lillian Disney, attributed quote does not appear in historical records but rather in many inspirational retellings.
7. George Lucas, "Dreams are extremely important. You can't do it unless you imagine it," attributed quote, Goodreads, accessed August 14, 2025, https://www.goodreads.com/quotes/369377-dreams-are-extremely-important-you-can-t-do-it-unless-you. *Note: This quote is commonly attributed to George Lucas but has not been verified through primary sources.*
8. Ken Kesey, "You don't lead by pointing and telling people some place to go. You lead by going to that place and making a case," attributed quote, Goodreads, accessed August 14, 2025, https://www.goodreads.com/quotes/7572751-you-don-t-lead-by-pointing-and-telling-people-some-place. *Note: This quote is commonly attributed to Ken Kesey but has not been verified through primary sources.*
9. John C. Maxwell, "You build trust with others each time you do what you say you will do," LinkedIn, accessed

August 14, 2025, https://www.linkedin.com/posts/officialjohnmaxwell_you-build-trust-with-others-each-time-you-activity-7330014612269973505-PQj9/.

CHAPTER 3

1. Henry Drummond, *Pax Vobiscum: And the Greatest Thing in the World* (Pollard Publishing Company, 1891), 27.
2. Billy Wilson, *Father Cry: Healing Your Heart and the Hearts of Those You Love* (ORU Press, 2025).
3. Melania Trump, "Fostering the Future," Be Best Initiative, accessed August 14, 2025, https://www.melaniatrump.com/pages/fostering-the-future.

CHAPTER 4

1. Dennis Bennett and Rita Bennett, *The Holy Spirit and You* (Bridge Logos, 1989).

CHAPTER 6

1. Ken Blanchard, *The Heart of a Leader* (David C. Cook, 2010). *Note: The quote "The heart of great leadership is a leader's great heart" is widely attributed to Blanchard and reflects the themes of this book, though it does not appear verbatim in the text.*
2. Laura Huang, "How CEOs Hone and Harness Their Intuition," *Harvard Business Review*, July 2025, https://hbr.org/2025/07/how-ceos-hone-and-harness-their-intuition.
3. Mark Miller, *The Heart of Leadership: Becoming a Leader People Want to Follow* (Berrett-Koehler Publishers, 2013).

4. Dwight D. Eisenhower, *Public Papers of the Presidents of the United States: Dwight D. Eisenhower, 1954* (US Government Printing Office, 1960).
5. "Ray Kroc Quotes," Goodreads, accessed August 14, 2025, https://www.goodreads.com/quotes/332832-the-quality-of-a-leader-is-reflected-in-the-standards. *Note: This quote is widely attributed to Ray Kroc, though no verified primary source confirms its origin.*
6. "Celebrating 75 Years of the Modesto Manifesto," Billy Graham Library, accessed August 14, 2025, https://billygrahamlibrary.org/blog-celebrating-75-years-of-the-modesto-manifesto/.
7. "Keep Your Fears to Yourself, but Share Your Courage with Others," Goodreads, accessed August 14, 2025, https://www.goodreads.com/quotes/22734-keep-your-fears-to-yourself-but-share-your-courage-with. *Note: This quote is widely attributed to Robert Louis Stevnson, though no verified primary source confirms its origin.*
8. "Wherever You Go, Go with All Your Heart," Goodreads, accessed August 14, 2025, https://www.goodreads.com/quotes/22734-keep-your-fears-to-yourself-but-share-your-courage-with. *Note: This quote is widely attributed to Confucius, though no verified primary source confirms its origin.*
9. "James Gibbons Quotes," A-Z Quotes, accessed August 14, 2025, https://www.azquotes.com/author/24400-James_Gibbons. *Note: This quote is widely attributed to James Gibbons, though no verified primary source confirms its origin.*
10. Rick Warren, *The Purpose-Driven Life: What on Earth Am I Here For?* (Zondervan, 2002), 148.

11. Lolly Daskal, "The Best Leaders Are Humble Leaders," Lolly Daskal, accessed August 14, 2025, https://www.lollydaskal.com/leadership/thebestleadersarehumble/.
12. "People Don't Care How Much You Know Until They Know How Much You Care," accessed September 4, 2025, https://www.goodreads.com/quotes/34690-people-don-t-care-how-much-you-know-until-they-know. *Note: This attribution is widely circulated but not verified in Roosevelt's documented speeches or writings.*
13. Movieclips, "Les Misérables (2012)–I Dreamed a Dream Scene (1/10)," YouTube video, 4:43, January 2, 2013, https://www.youtube.com/watch?v=ulJXiB5i_q0[1].

CHAPTER 7

1. INSEAD Emerging Markets Institute, Universum, The HEAD Foundation, and MIT Leadership Centre, "Generations Series: Building Leaders for the Next Decade," INSEAD, accessed August 14, 2025, https://www.insead.edu/sites/default/files/assets/dept/centres/emi/docs/generations-series-building-leaders-for-the-next-decade.pdf.
2. JRR Tolkien, *The Fellowship of the Ring* (Houghton Mifflin Harcourt, 2005).
3. Walter Lippmann, "The Final Test of a Leader," *New York Herald Tribune*, April 14, 1945, quoted in *Oxford Essential Quotations*, 4th ed., accessed August 14, 2025, https://www.oxfordreference.com/display/10.1093/acref/9780191826719.001.0001/q-oro-ed4-00006726.

CHAPTER 8

1. Mark Twain, *A Connecticut Yankee in King Arthur's Court* (Charles L. Webster & Co., 1889).
2. Chris Erskine, "Yogi Berra Turns 90: A Look Back at His Most Memorable Quotes," *Los Angeles Times*, May 12, 2015, https://www.latimes.com/sports/sportsnow/la-sp-sn-yogi-berra-turns-90-quotes-20150512-story.html.
3. Theodore Roosevelt, "Address at the Prize Day Exercises, Groton School," American Literature, May 24, 1904, accessed August 14, 2025, https://americanliterature.com/history/theodore-roosevelt/Speech/address-at-the-prize-day-exercises-groton-school.
4. Brian Tracy, *The Gift of Self-Confidence* (Jaico Publishing House, 1998).
5. Peter F. Drucker, *Management* (Routledge, 1974), 123, https://www.taylorfrancis.com/books/mono/10.4324/9780080939063/management-peter-drucker.
6. Maxwell Leadership, "3 Pillars of Team Development Success," Maxwell Leadership, November 14, 2023, https://www.maxwellleadership.com/blog/3-pillars-team-development-success/.
7. Ken Blanchard, "No One of Us Is As Smart As All of Us," Ken Blanchard Books, May 25, 2022, https://www.kenblanchardbooks.com/no-one-of-us-is-as-smart-as-all-of-us/.
8. Ronald Reagan, "Leadership," Ronald Reagan Presidential Foundation & Institute, December 14, 1975, accessed August 14, 2025, https://www.reaganfoundation.org/ronald-reagan/quotes/leadership.

9. Stephanie Moulton Sarkis, "A Good Boss Is a Good Leader: Quotes," *Psychology Today*, May 14, 2011, https://www.psychologytoday.com/us/blog/here-there-and-everywhere/201105/good-boss-is-good-leader-quotes. *Note: This quote is widely attributed to Robert Jarvik, though no primary source verifies.*
10. Donald L. Wasson, "The Army of Alexander the Great," *World History Encyclopedia*, April 4, 2014, accessed August 14, 2025, https://www.worldhistory.org/article/676/the-army-of-alexander-the-great/.

CHAPTER 9

1. Vince Lombardi, *Motivation Lombardi Style*, compiled by Successories Inc. staff (Successories Inc., 1998).
2. *Liber Facetiarum: Being a Collection of Curious and Interesting Anecdotes* (D. Akenhead and Sons, 1809), 182.
3. "Thinking Influences Performance," Ziglar.com, accessed August 14, 2025, https://www.ziglar.com/inspiration/thinking-influences-performance/.
4. Viktor E. Frankl, *Man's Search for Meaning*, trans. Ilse Lasch (Beacon Press, 2006).
5. Johnny Creasong, "Your Attitude Will Determine Your Altitude," SermonCentral, November 28, 2017, https://sermoncentral.com/sermons/your-attitude-will-determine-your-altitude-johnny-creasong-sermon-on-christian-disciplines-48265.

CHAPTER 10

1. Travis Bradberry, "Emotional Intelligence 2.0 Step by Step," TalentSmartEQ, November 4, 2024, https://www.talentsmarteq.com/emotional-intelligence-2-0-step-by-step/.
2. John F. Kennedy, "Remarks Prepared for Delivery at the Trade Mart in Dallas, TX, November 22, 1963" (undelivered), John F. Kennedy Presidential Library and Museum, https://www.jfklibrary.org/archives/other-resources/john-f-kennedy-speeches/dallas-tx-trade-mart-undelivered-19631122.

CHAPTER 11

1. Gina A. Zurlo, ed., *World Christian Database* (Brill, 2025).
2. Adapted from original illustration by Hal Knight.
3. Jonathan Edwards, "Some Thoughts Concerning the Present Revival in New England," in *The Works of Jonathan Edwards* (1834; reprint, Banner of Truth, 1974), 1:376.
4. R. D. Chatham, *Fasting: A Biblical-Historical Study* (Bridge, 1987), 91, quoting Arthur Wallis, *God's Chosen Fast* (Christian Literature Crusade, 1993), 34–35.
5. "1727: Great Awakening and Whitefield," Revival Library, accessed September 29, 2025, https://revival-library.org/histories/1727-great-awakening-and-whitefield/.
6. Joseph Belcher, *George Whitefield: A Biography, with Special Reference to His Labors in America* (American Tract Society, 1857), 182.
7. Harry Stout, *The Divine Dramatist: George Whitefield and the Rise of Modern Evangelicalism* (Eerdmans, 1991), 128–130; see also, 152–153.

8. Iain H. Murray, *The Great Awakening in America: Religious Revival in the Late Eighteenth Century* (Moody Press, 1955).
9. Michael L. Brown, *Saving a Sick America: A Prescription for Moral and Cultural Transformation* (Thomas Nelson, 2017), 183.
10. Tony Cauchi, "The Second Great Awakening–1792," Revival Library, accessed August 14, 2025, https://revival-library.org/histories/1792-the-second-great-awakening/.
11. US Census Bureau, *1950 Census of Population: Volume 2, Characteristics of the Population* (US Government Printing Office), chap. 2.
12. Amy Lifson, "Like at Cane Ridge," *Humanities* 45, no. 4 (Fall 2024), National Endowment for the Humanities, accessed August 14, 2025, https://www.neh.gov/article/cane-ridge.
13. Paul K. Conkin, *Cane Ridge: America's Pentecost* (University of Wisconsin Press, 1990).
14. *Register of Kentucky State Historical Society*, 19, no. 56 (May 1921): 9–30, Kentucky Historical Society, https://www.jstor.org/stable/23369550.
15. Mark Galli, ed., *Christian History*, no. 45: "Camp Meetings & Circuit Riders: Frontier Revivals—Revival at Cane Ridge" (1995).
16. Galli, ed., "Camp Meetings & Circuit Riders."
17. Conkin, *Cane Ridge, America's Pentecost*, 1990.
18. Thomas S. Kidd, "A Brief History of the Altar Call," The Gospel Coalition, accessed August 14, 2025, https://www.thegospelcoalition.org/blogs/evangelical-history/a-brief-history-of-the-altar-call/.
19. Henry H. Knight III, ed., *Wesleyan, Holiness, and Pentecostal*

Visions of the New Creation (Pickwick Publications, 2010).

20. Agnes N. Ozman, "My Personal Testimony of Being the First Person to Receive the Holy Ghost," *The Apostolic Faith,* April 1951; *Apostolic Archives,* accessed September 5, 2025, https://www.apostolicarchives.com/articles/article/8801925/173171.htm.

21. Charles F. Parham, "The Latter Rain," *The Apostolic Faith*, April 1951, reprinted at *Apostolic Archives,* https://www.apostolicarchives.com/articles/article/8801925/173163.htm.

22. Harold Hunter, "Tongues-Speech: A Patristic Analysis," *Journal of the Evangelical Theological Society* 23, no. 2 (June 1980): 125–37.

23. James R. Goff Jr., *Fields White Unto Harvest: Charles F. Parham and the Missionary Origins of Pentecostalism* (University of Arkansas Press, 1988).

24. Cecil M. Robeck, Jr., *The Azusa Street Mission and Revival: The Birth of the Global Pentecostal Movement* (Thomas Nelson, 2006), 47.

25. Larry Jay Martin, *The Life and Ministry of William J. Seymour: And a History of the Azusa Street Revival* (Christian Life Books, 1999).

26. Robeck, *The Azusa Street Mission and Revival,* 63–64.

27. Robeck, *The Azusa Street Mission and Revival,* 63–68.

28. Robeck, *The Azusa Street Mission and Revival,* 69–71.

29. Robeck, *The Azusa Street Mission and Revival*, 74.

30. *Los Angeles Times,* April 18, 1906, 17.

31. Michael J. McClymond, "Azusa Street Commentary and Excerpts," *Christian History Magazine,* no. 153 (2024), Christian History Institute, https://christianhistoryinstitute.org/magazine/article/ch153-Azusa-commentary.

32. McClymond, "Azusa Street Commentary and Excerpts."
33. *Los Angeles Times*, "Azusa Street Revival," Scroll Publishing Company, https://scrollpublishing.com/azusa-street-revival/.
34. Dennis J. Bennett, *Nine O'clock in the Morning* (Bridge-Logos, 1970), 73.
35. Zurlo, *World Christian Database*.
36. Zurlo, *World Christian Database*.
37. Todd M. Johnson and Gina A. Zurlo, *Introducing Spirit-Empowered Christianity: The Global Pentecostal and Charismatic Movements in the 21st Century* (ORU Press, 2020).
38. Vinson Synan and Billy Wilson, *As the Waters Cover the Sea: The Story of Empowered21 and the Movement It Serves* (Empowered21 Press, 2021).

CHAPTER 12

1. Story told to Dr. Wilson by Cameron Fisher, son of Dr. Robert Fisher.

CHAPTER 13

1. Zig Ziglar, "Failure Is a Detour, Not a Dead-End Street," Ziglar.com, accessed August 14, 2025, https://www.ziglar.com/quotes/failure-is-a-detour-not-a-dead-end-street/.
2. Max Lucado, "God Uses Failures," MaxLucado.com, accessed August 14, 2025, https://maxlucado.com/listen/uses-failures/.
3. Joyce Meyer, "Don't Be Afraid to Try Something New," Joyce Meyer Ministries, accessed August 22, 2025, https://joycemeyer.org/en/Grow-Your-Faith/Articles/dont-be-afraid-to-try-something-new.

4. Bob Goff, *Love Does: Discover a Secretly Incredible Life in an Ordinary World* (Thomas Nelson, 2012), 29.
5. Associated Press, "Rory McIlroy Wins Masters Playoff to Complete Career Grand Slam," PGA TOUR, April 13, 2025, https://www.pgatour.com/article/news/daily-wrapup/2025/04/13/masters-tournament-augusta-national-storylines-leaderboard-recap-rory-mcilroy-dechambeau-scheffler-aberg-justin-rose.
6. David W. Duffy, "Why Did Apple's Board Fire Steve Jobs in 1985?" Corporate Governance Institute, accessed August 15, 2025, https://www.thecorporategovernanceinstitute.com/insights/case-studies/why-did-apples-board-fire-steve-jobs-in-1985/.
7. William Gallagher, "Steve Jobs Returned to Apple on July 9, 1997," AppleInsider, July 10, 2018, https://appleinsider.com/articles/18/07/10/gil-amelio-resigned-at-apple-ceo-21-years-ago-paving-the-way-for-steve-jobs-ascension-as-ceo.
8. Allison Johnson, "Apple Now Has More Than 2 Billion Active Devices," *The Verge*, February 2, 2023, https://www.theverge.com/2023/2/2/23583501/apple-iphone-ipad-active-2-billion-devices-q1-2023.
9. Thomas A. Edison, quoted in F. L. Dyer and T. C. Martin, *Edison: His Life and Inventions* (Harper & Brothers, 1910), as cited in *Oxford Essential Quotations*, 4th ed., ed. Susan Ratcliffe (Oxford University Press, 2016), https://www.oxfordreference.com/display/10.1093/acref/9780191826719.001.0001/q-oro-ed4-00003960.
10. Jonathan Rosen, "Oh, the Places He Went! When Dr. Seuss Took His Whimsy to War," *New York Times*, July 3, 1999,

https://archive.nytimes.com/www.nytimes.com/library/books/070399seuss-tank.html.
11. "Babe Ruth Career Stats," ESPN, accessed August 15, 2025, https://www.espn.com/mlb/player/stats/_/id/27035/babe-ruth.
12. Michael Jordan, "Michael Jordan," *Forbes*, accessed August 15, 2025, https://www.forbes.com/profile/michael-jordan/.
13. National Park Service, "Thomas Lincoln," National Park Service, last modified May 31, 2024, https://www.nps.gov/people/thomas-lincoln.htm.
14. NPS, *Life of Lincoln*.
15. National Park Service, "Sarah Lincoln Grigsby," National Park Service, modified January 12, 2022, https://www.nps.gov/people/sarah-lincoln-grigsby.htm.
16. Abraham Lincoln Online, "First Political Announcement," Abraham Lincoln Online, accessed September 5, 2025, https://www.abrahamlincolnonline.org/lincoln/speeches/1832.htm.
17. Papers of Abraham Lincoln Digital Library, "Lincoln & Berry," Papers of Abraham Lincoln, accessed September 5, 2025, https://papersofabrahamlincoln.org/organizations/LI25459.
18. National Park Service, "Lincoln in the Illinois State Legislature," accessed September 4, 2025, https://www.nps.gov/articles/000/lincoln-in-the-illinois-state-legislature.htm.
19. Kentucky's Abraham Lincoln, Kentucky Historical Society, February 2008, https://apps.legislature.ky.gov/LegislativeMoments/moments09RS/web/Lincoln%20moments%204.pdf.
20. Abraham Lincoln Online, "Lincoln's Failures," accessed

September 5, 2025, https://www.abrahamlincolnonline.org/lincoln/education/failures.htm.

21. Abraham Lincoln Online, "Timeline of Abraham Lincoln's Political Career," accessed September 5, 2025, https://www.abrahamlincolnonline.org/lincoln/education/polbrief.htm.bak.

22. National Park Service, "Resource Material Guide," Abraham Lincoln Birthplace National Historical Park Kentucky, August 25, 2025, https://www.nps.gov/abli/learn/education/resource-material-guide.htm

23. NPS, "Resource Material Guide."

24. Abraham Lincoln Online, "Lincoln's Failures," Abraham Lincoln Online, accessed September 5, 2025, https://www.abrahamlincolnonline.org/lincoln/education/failures.htm.

25. Abraham Lincoln Association, "Timeline," Abraham Lincoln Association, accessed September 5, 2025, https://www.abrahamlincoln.org/themes/timelines/printable-timeline/index.html.

26. Abraham Lincoln Association, "Timeline."

27. Abraham Lincoln Online, "Lincoln's Failures."

28. National Park Service, "The Lincoln-Douglas Debates of 1858," Lincoln Home National Historic Site Illinois, accessed September 4, 2025, https://www.nps.gov/liho/learn/historyculture/debates.htm.

29. Abraham Lincoln Association, "Timeline."

30. Bill Hybels, "Reading Your Gauges," *Christianity Today*, May 19, 2004, https://www.christianitytoday.com/2004/05/reading-your-gauges/.

CHAPTER 14

1. Brian Tracy, "117 Leadership Quotes for Inspiration," BrianTracy.com, accessed August 19, 2025, https://www.briantracy.com/blog/leadership-success/leadership-quotes-for-inspiration/.
2. Zack Friedman, "Here Are 10 Genius Quotes From Warren Buffett," *Forbes*, October 4, 2018, https://www.forbes.com/sites/zackfriedman/2018/10/04/warren-buffett-best-quotes/.
3. John Wooden and Steve Jamison, *Wooden: A Lifetime of Observations and Reflections On and Off the Court* (McGraw-Hill, 1997), 67.
4. Amitabh Ray, "Human Knowledge Doubling Every 12 Hours," LinkedIn Pulse, October 22, 2020, https://www.linkedin.com/pulse/human-knowledge-doubling-every-12-hours-amitabh-ray/.
5. World Economic Forum, "Future of Jobs Report 2025," accessed August 19, 2025, https://reports.weforum.org/docs/WEF_Future_of_Jobs_Report_2025.pdf.
6. John Wesley, *The Complete Works of John Wesley*, vol. 1, *Journals 1735–1745* (AGES Software, 1997), 228, https://media.sabda.org/alkitab-10/LIBRARY/COLLECT/WESLEY_C/WES_WW01.PDF.

www.ingramcontent.com/pod-product-compliance
Lightning Source LLC
Chambersburg PA
BHW050527100526
14581CB00009B/153/J